Collins Primary Maths
Pupil Book 1

Series Editor: Peter Clarke

Authors: Andrew Edmondson, Elizabeth Jurgensen,
Jeanette Mumford, Sandra Roberts

Contents

Topic	Objective	Pages
Place value, ordering and rounding/Using a calculator	To multiply and divide decimals mentally by 10 or 100, and integers by 1000 and explain the effect To consolidate rounding an integer to the nearest 10, 100 or 1000 To develop calculator skills and use a calculator effectively To order a given set of positive and negative integers	4–5, 6–7, 8–9
Understanding multiplication and division/Rapid recall of multiplication and division facts	To consolidate knowing by heart multiplication facts up to 10×10 To derive quickly division facts corresponding to tables up to 10×10	10–11
Mental calculation strategies ($\times$ and $\div$)	To use related facts and doubling or halving. For example: double or halve the most significant digit first To use related facts and doubling or halving. For example: to multiply by 25, multiply by 100 then divide by 4; double or halve the most significant digit first; find the $\times 24$ table by doubling the $\times 6$ table twice To multiply mentally any two-digit number to 50 by a single-digit number	12–13, 14–15, 16–17 18–19
Pencil and paper procedures ($\times$)	To approximate first. Use informal pencil and paper methods to support, record or explain multiplications To extend written methods to short multiplication of numbers involving decimals To estimate by approximating (round to the nearest 10, 100 or 1000) then check result	20–21, 22–23 24–25, 26–27
Problems involving "real life" and money/Making decisions	To identify and use appropriate operations (including combinations of operations) to solve word problems involving numbers and quantities based on "real life" or money, using one or more steps	28–29, 102–103 104–105
Fractions, decimals, percentages, ratio and proportion	To change a fraction such as $3\frac{3}{8}$ to equivalent mixed number $4\frac{1}{8}$, and vice versa	30–31
	To recognise relationships between fractions: for example, that $\frac{1}{10}$ is ten times $\frac{1}{100}$, and $\frac{1}{16}$ is half of $\frac{1}{8}$	32–33
	To reduce a fraction to its simplest form by cancelling common factors in the numerator and denominator	34–35
	To know what each digit represents in a number with up to three decimal places	36–37
	To recognise the equivalence between the decimal and fraction forms of one half, one quarter, three quarters, one eighth…and tenths, hundredths and thousandths	38–39
	To use decimal notation for tenths and hundredths in calculations, and tenths, hundredths and thousandths when recording measurements	40–41
	To understand percentage as the number of parts in every 100	42–43
	To find simple percentages of small whole number quantities	44–45
	To solve simple problems involving ratio and proportion	46–47, 48–49

Handling data	To use the language associated with probability to discuss events, including those with equally likely outcomes	50–51, 52–53, 54–55
	To solve a problem by representing, extracting and interpreting data in tables, charts, graphs and diagrams, including those generated by a computer, for example: bar charts with grouped discrete data	56–57, 58–59, 60–61, 62–63, 64–65
	To find the mode and range of a set of data	
	To begin to find the median of a set of data	
Shape and space: (2D)/ Reasoning and generalising about shapes/(position and direction)/(reflective symmetry, reflection and translation)	To describe and visualise properties of solid shapes such as parallel or perpendicular faces or edges	66–67
	To classify quadrilaterals, using criteria such as parallel sides, equal angles, equal sides …	68–69, 70–71, 72–73
	To read and plot co-ordinates in all four quadrants	74–75
	To recognise where a shape will be after two translations	76–77, 78–79
	To solve mathematical problems or puzzles, recognise and explain patterns and relationships, generalise and predict. Suggest extensions asking "What if …?"	82–83, 84–85
Measures: (area and perimeter)	To calculate the perimeter of simple compound shapes that can be split into rectangles	80–81
Measures: (time)/Problems involving "real life" or measures	To appreciate different times around the world	86–87
Measures: (length)/Making decisions	To use, read and write standard metric units of length (km, m, cm, mm), including their abbreviations and relationships between them	88–89
	To convert smaller to larger units (e.g. m to km, cm or mm to m) and vice versa	90–91
	To know imperial units (mile)	92–93
	To know rough equivalents of miles and kilometres	
Problems involving measures (length)	To identify and use appropriate operations (including combinations of operations) to solve word problems involving numbers and quantities based on measures (length), using one or more steps	94–95
Mental calculation strategies (+ and –)	To find a difference by counting up	96–97
	To add or subtract the nearest multiple of 10, 100 or 1000 then adjust	
Pencil and paper procedures (+ and –)/ Checking results of calculations	To extend written methods to column addition/subtraction involving decimals	98–99, 100–101
Properties of numbers and number sequences	To recognise squares of numbers to at least 12×12	106–107, 108–109
	To recognise and extend number sequences such as the sequence of triangular numbers, 1, 3, 6, 10, 15…	
	To recognise and extend number sequences such as the sequence of square numbers	110–111, 112–113
Reasoning and generalising about numbers	To solve mathematical problems or puzzles, recognise and explain patterns and relationships, generalise and predict. Suggest extensions asking "What if…?"	114–115

Changing places

Practice

1 What is the place value of the red digits?

a 586 214 b 720 963 c 465 769
d 327 125 e 902 824 f 3 684 977
g 2 962 205 h 4 073 617 i 8 831 429

2 Now choose two of the numbers and write them out in words.

3 Copy and complete the multiplication calculations.

a 30 × ▮ = 300

b 45 × ▮ = 450

c 37 × 100 = ▮

d 21 × ▮ = 21 000

e ▮ × 1000 = 86 000

f 124 × ▮ = 12 400

g ▮ × 10 = 2630

h 191 × 100 = ▮

i ▮ × 1000 = 506 000

j ▮ × 10 = 7120

k 6·2 × 10 = ▮

l 8·7 × 100 = ▮

m 19·4 × ▮ = 194

n 67·26 × ▮ = 6726

o ▮ × 10 = 743·9

4 Copy and complete the division calculations.

a 64 000 ÷ 10 = ▮

b 7800 ÷ 100 = ▮

c 8100 ÷ ▮ = 810

d 9600 ÷ ▮ = 96

e ▮ ÷ 100 = 580

f 42 000 ÷ ▮ = 42

g 3000 ÷ ▮ = 3

h ▮ ÷ 1000 = 6·7

i 910 ÷ 100 = ▮

j ▮ ÷ 100 = 8·63

k 721 ÷ 10 = ▮

l 578 ÷ ▮ = 5·78

m ▮ ÷ 10 = 6·7

n 28·3 ÷ 10 = ▮

o 165 ÷ ▮ = 1·65

5 Explain how to multiply and divide by 10, 100 and 1000.

4

Refresher

Example
7262
I know the 7 is 7000

1 What is the place value of the red digits?

a 6581   b 9123   c 7164

d 3854   e 28 361   f 35 684

g 24 362   h 62 146   i 78 205

Draw a place value chart if it helps!

Hth	Th	H	T	U
		7	2	6	5

2 Now choose two of the numbers and write them out in words.

3 Multiply these numbers by 10.

Example
63 × 10 = 630

a 58   b 72

c 61   d 94

e 751   f 361

g 821   h 500

i 6200   j 5641

k 7013   l 5267

4 Divide these numbers by 10.

Example
50 ÷ 10 = 5

a 90   b 20

c 60   d 250

e 170   f 800

g 960   h 470

i 2650   j 3820

k 9800   l 7260

5 Multiply these numbers by 100

a 45

b 38

c 475

d 200

e 634

Example
67 × 100 = 6700

6 Divide these numbers by 100.

a 400

b 600

c 4500

d 3100

e 40 000

Example
900 ÷ 100 = 9

Challenge

Use multiplying and dividing by 10 and 100 to help work out these problems.

1 How many £10 notes in £130, £1300, £13 000?

2 How many 10p coins in £145, £1450, £14 500?

3 Explain how you worked out the answers.

Round, multiply and divide

Practice

1 Round these numbers to the nearest multiple of 10, 100 and 1000.

    a 73 138   **b** 62 267   **c** 15 509   **d** 27 823   **e** 49 077

    f 487 273   **g** 931 862   **h** 518 963   **i** 297 028   **j** 499 763

2 Decide whether to multiply or divide by 10, 100 or 1000 to change the first number to the second.

    a 547 ☐ 54 700   **b** 273 ☐ 27 300

    c 486 ☐ 486 000   **d** 6·83 ☐ 683

    e 8679 ☐ 867 900   **f** 8 000 000 ☐ 8000

    g 9680 ☐ 96·8   **h** 490 000 ☐ 490

    i 516 000 ☐ 516   **j** 931 ☐ 9·31

3 Use a calculator to carry out the following operations on each number.
Record the number the calculator displays after each operation.

    × 10 × 10 × 10 × 10 × 10 × 10 ÷10 ÷10 ÷10 ÷10 ÷10 ÷10

    a 0·06

    b 7·2

    c 1·94

    d 3·07

    e 5·68

Example

0·03 × 10 = 0·3

0·3 × 10 = 3

3 × 10 = 30

30000 ÷ 10 = 3000

3000 ÷ 10 = 300

300 ÷ 10 = 30

Now carry on dividing!

Remember

You can use the constant function for the division calculations.

Refresher

Example

| | nearest multiple of | | |
	10	100	1000
1483	1480	1500	1000

1 Round these numbers to the nearest multiple of 10, 100 and 1000.

  a 1762   b 2493   c 3527   d 5086   e 7315

  f 2378   g 4231   h 7567   i 5058   j 1920

2 Work out these pairs of calculations.

  a $62 \times 10 \times 10$ b $76 \times 10 \times 10$ c $21 \times 10 \times 10 \times 10$ d $47 \times 10 \times 10 \times 10$
     62×100 76×100 21×1000 47×1000

  e 23×1000 f $400 \div 10 \div 10$ g $3900 \div 10 \div 10$ h $6720 \div 10 \div 10$
     $23 \times 10 \times 10 \times 10$ $400 \div 100$ $3900 \div 100$ $6720 \div 100$

  i $8000 \div 10 \div 10 \div 10$ j $7200 \div 10 \div 10 \div 10$
    $8000 \div 1000$ $7200 \div 1000$

3 Use a calculator to carry out the following operations on each number. Record the number the calculator displays after each operation.

Remember You can use the constant function for the division calculations.

$\times 10$ $\times 10$ $\times 10$ $\times 10$ $\div 10$ $\div 10$ $\div 10$ $\div 10$

  a 78   b 41

  c 32   d 149

  e 367   f 53

Example
$67 \times 10 = 670$
$670 \times 10 = 6700$
$6700 \times 10 = 67\,000$
$670\,000 \div 10 = 67\,000$
$67\,000 \div 10 = 6700$
$6700 \div 10 = 670$

Challenge

Use multiplying and dividing by 10, 100 and 1000 to solve these problems.

a How many times larger than 34 is 34 000?
b How many times larger than 2·5 is 2500?
c How many times larger than 148 is 14 800?
d How many times smaller than 310 000 is 31?
e How many times smaller than 894 is 89·4?
f How many times smaller than 4000 is 0·04?

Positive and negative temperatures

Practice

Use the thermometer to help you work out these questions.
Record your answers as calculations.

a The temperature is 7 °C. It drops by 9 degrees.
What is the temperature now?

b At night the temperature was −6 °C, in the day it was 1°C.
What was the difference between the temperatures?

c The temperature is −11 °C. It rises by 4 degrees. What is
the temperature now?

d The temperature is −2 °C. If it gets 5 degrees colder what
will the temperature be?

e The highest temperature this week was 3 °C. The lowest
temperature was −5 °C. What was the difference between
the highest and lowest temperatures?

f The temperature at the North Pole is −20 °C. How much
will the temperature need to rise to be −5 °C?

g The temperature now is −1 °C. The weather forecast
predicts that later on it will be −13 °C. How much will the
temperature drop?

h In London the temperature is −1 °C and in Moscow it is
−9 °C. How much colder is Moscow than London?

i The temperature is −6 °C. It rises by 14 degrees. What is
the temperature now?

j The temperature now is −4 °C. Tomorrow it will be
8 degrees warmer. What will be the temperature then?

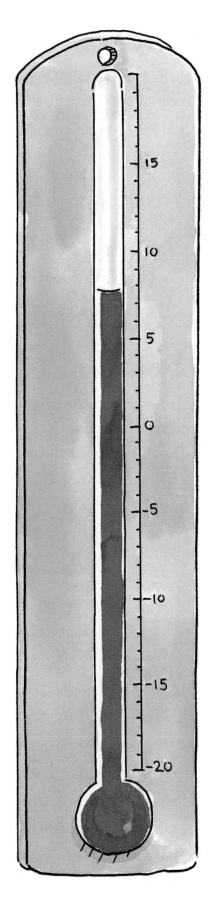

Refresher

1 Order these numbers from smallest to largest.

a 9 −5 3 −4 −1 7 −10 6
b 0 −14 −5 8 10 −3 2 −2
c −21 −7 15 7 −3 12 −8 1
d −4 −8 −2 0 −9 −1 3 5
e −15 −31 −28 −6 −22 −11 −29 −25

2 Use the thermometer in the Practice section to help you work out these questions.

Remember

Remember the numbers below zero are negative numbers.

a The temperature is 2 °C. It drops by 3 degrees. What is the temperature now?
b The temperature is 4 °C. It drops by 7 degrees. What is the temperature now?
c The temperature is 5 °C. It drops by 9 degrees. What is the temperature now?
d The temperature is 1 °C. It drops by 10 degrees. What is the temperature now?
e The temperature is 3 °C. It drops by 6 degrees. What is the temperature now?
f The temperature is −4 °C. It drops by 2 degrees. What is the temperature now?
g The temperature is −7 °C. It rises by 3 degrees. What is the temperature now?
h The temperature is −10 °C. It rises by 6 degrees. What is the temperature now?

Challenge

Work out these calculations.

a 4 − 9   b 3 − 15   c 0 − 7   d 2 − 12
e 1 − 13   f −9 + 3   g −10 + 9   h −14 + 5
i −20 + 7   j −18 + 12   k −12 + 6   l 0 − 12

Taxi journey problems

Practice

Total Taxi Services
Getting you to the airport on time

From your door to	Heathrow Airport	Gatwick Airport	Stansted Airport
1 person	£10	£12	£15
2 people	£9 each	£11 each	£12 each
3 to 5 people	£7 each	£9 each	£8 each

Here is the guide to prices the Total Taxi Services uses when transporting people to London airports. Use it to help you answer these questions.

a How much for 2 people to travel to Gatwick Airport in 1 taxi?

b What is the total cost for 4 people to travel to Stansted Airport in 1 taxi?

c The driver charged 5 people £42 to travel in 1 taxi to Heathrow Airport. Was he correct?

d 4 people took a taxi to the airport. It cost them £36. Where did they go to?

e 3 people took a taxi to Stansted. The driver gave them £26 change. How much money did they give him?

f Is it cheaper for 2 people to take a taxi to Stansted or 3 people to take a taxi to Gatwick?

g How much money does the taxi to Heathrow make by taking 2 people? 3 people? 4 people? 5 people?

h 4 taxis each take 1 person to Gatwick Airport. How much would each person save if they went in 1 taxi?

i 8 people take separate taxis to Gatwick. How much is spent in taxi fares?

j 8 people travel in 2 taxis to Heathrow. How much does each taxi cost? What is the total bill?

k 9 people travel to Stansted. What is the cheapest way to get there?

l 6 friends travelled to Gatwick. What is the cheapest way to get there?

Refresher

Copy and complete each number square. Multiply the numbers on the two corners to find the number in the middle.

Example
$6 \times 5 = 30$

a

6	30	5
7		4

b

3		9
6		8

c

7		5
9		8

d

11		8
3		7

e

12		6
4		6

f

11		5
4		9

g

	36	
	64	

h

	56	
		48
7		

i

		9
54		
	72	

Challenge

Product magic squares

Look at this magic square. The numbers are made by multiplying instead of adding.

36	16	3
1	12	144
48	9	4

1 What are the properties of a product magic square? (Hint: The number in the middle is important!)

2 Will the product magic square work if the rules are not followed?

3 Copy and complete these product magic squares.

a

		2
1	14	196
98		

b

		4
1	8	
16		2

Doubles and halves splash

Practice

Look at the instruction and double or halve each number as you go down the slide.

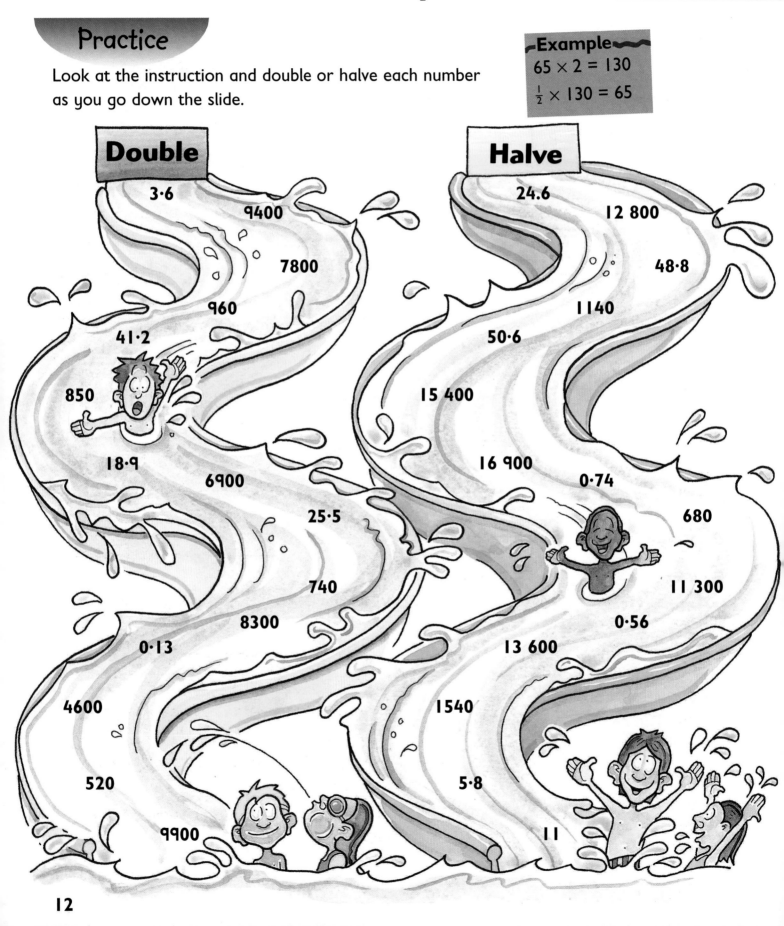

Double

3·6
9400
7800
960
41·2
850
18·9
6900
25·5
740
8300
0·13
4600
520
9900

Halve

24.6
12 800
48·8
1140
50·6
15 400
16 900
0·74
680
11 300
0·56
13 600
1540
5·8
11

Refresher

Look at the instruction on each machine. Double or halve each number going into the machine to get a new number.

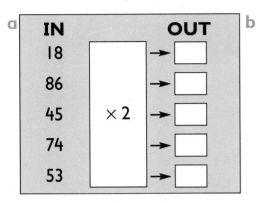

a

IN		OUT
18		
86		
45	× 2	
74		
53		

b

IN		OUT
92		
30		
64	$\frac{1}{2}$	
26		
52		

c

IN		OUT
82		
37		
95	× 2	
29		
48		

d

IN		OUT
74		
		39
	$\frac{1}{2}$	48
64		
56		

e

IN		OUT
39		
63		
	× 2	50
		80
		90

f

IN		OUT
98		
74		
62	÷ 2	

Challenge

Play the halving game

You need:
- paper and pencil
- 20 number cards between 1 and 40
- minute timer

14 → 7 → 3·5 → 1·75

What to do

Play with a partner

1 Place the number cards face down in a pile. Turn over the top card.

2 Both players write the number down.

3 Start the minute timer.

4 Halve the number and keep halving your answer until the minute is up.

5 Compare your answers. The player with the most correct answers scores 1 point.

6 The first player to reach 10 points is the winner.

Easy 25s

Practice

1 Look at the rule for multiplying by 50.
Use the rule to multiply these numbers by 50.

Rule

To × 50

first × 100

then ÷ 2

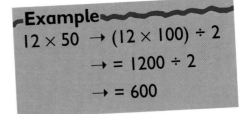

Example

$12 \times 50 \rightarrow (12 \times 100) \div 2$

$\rightarrow = 1200 \div 2$

$\rightarrow = 600$

a 17   b 64
c 32   d 25
e 28   f 50
g 82   h 39
i 76   j 91

2 Now look at the rule for multiplying by 25.
Use the rule to multiply these numbers by 25.

Example

$12 \times 25 \rightarrow (12 \times 100) \div 4$

$\rightarrow = 1200 \div 4$

$\rightarrow = 300$

Rule

To × 25

first × 100

then ÷ 4

a 16   b 48
c 32   d 24
e 44   f 26
g 34   h 50
i 60   j 38

$6 \times 25 = 150$

3 Multiply these numbers by 25, using the rule above.
Try to work out the answers in your head. Write the answer.

a 12   b 36   c 28   d 80

e 30   f 52   g 46   h 77

Refresher

Multiply the number shown on the calculator display by 100.
Write the new number.

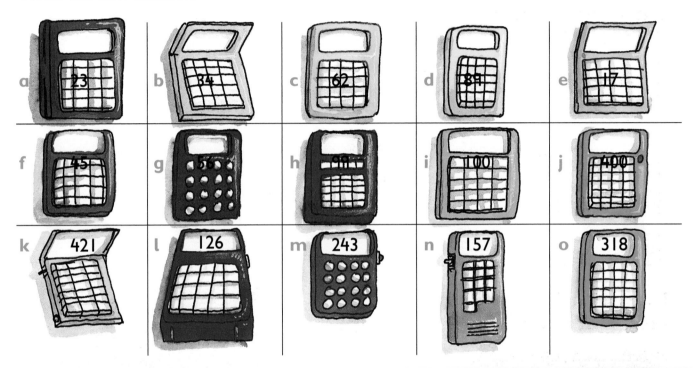

a 23　　b 34　　c 62　　d 89　　e 17

f 45　　g 56　　h 99　　i 100　　j 400

k 421　　l 126　　m 243　　n 157　　o 318

Challenge

Quick 25s game

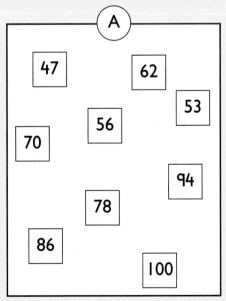

A

| 47 | 62 |
| 53 |
| 56 |
| 70 |
| 94 |
| 78 |
| 86 |
| 100 |

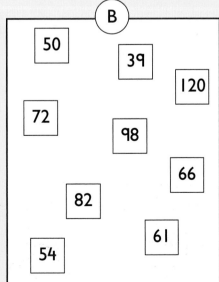

B

| 50 |
| 39 |
| 120 |
| 72 |
| 98 |
| 66 |
| 82 |
| 61 |
| 54 |

What to do

Play with a partner

1 One player uses the numbers in Box A. The other player uses the numbers in Box B.

2 Start at the same time and multiply each of the numbers by 25 in your head. Write the answer.

3 Who is the quickest? Swap boxes and play again, then check your answers.

Helpful doubles

Practice

Example
$$14 \times 24 = (14 \times 6) \times 2 \times 2$$
$$= (84 \times 2) \times 2$$
$$= 168 \times 2$$
$$= 336$$

1 Use the 6 times table and doubling to help you
find the answers when these numbers are multiplied by 24.

a 8   b 12   c 20   d 9   e 15

f 24   g 32   h 30   i 50   j 42

2 Find the answer to each number fact for 24 by
multiplying by 6, then doubling your answer twice.

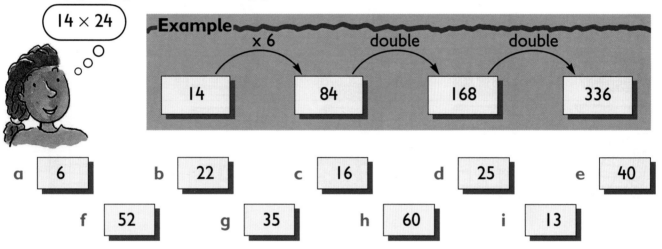

14 × 24

Example

	× 6		double		double	
14	→	84	→	168	→	336

a 6   b 22   c 16   d 25   e 40

f 52   g 35   h 60   i 13

3 There are other ways in which doubling can be used to
multiply large numbers. This is a method Russian peasants used.

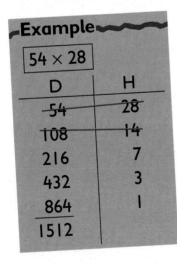

Example

54 × 28

D	H
~~54~~	~~28~~
~~108~~	~~14~~
216	7
432	3
864	1
1512	

Rule

1 Double one number, halve
the other, leaving out
halves, until you reach 1.

2 Look at the halving
column. Whenever an
even number appears,
cross out the numbers in
both columns.

3 Add the remaining numbers
in the doubling column to
get your answer.

Try these, then check your
answers with a calculator.

a 36 × 25

b 43 × 24

c 24 × 37

Refresher

Find the multiples of 6, then write a number fact for 6 that matches the number card.

Example
6   1 × 6 = 6

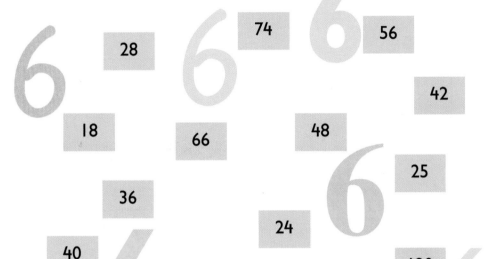

28   74   56   32   72

42   60   30

18   66   48

25

36   24   12   26

40   120   100

54   46

Challenge

Here are two more examples of multiplication where doubling has been used to help find the answer. For each one:

1 Decide what was done and write down how the method works.

2 Write down why the method works.

3 Try both methods to work out:

   a 46 × 24   b 47 × 28   c 26 × 32

4 Which method is better? Why?

Example 1

54 × 28

$54 \times 10 = 540$
$54 \times 20 = 1080$
$54 \times 30 = 1620$
$54 \times 2 \;\; = \;\; 108 -$
$54 \times 28 = 1512$

Example 2

54 × 28

$2 \times 54 \;\; = \;\; 108$
$4 \times 54 \;\; = \;\; 216$
$8 \times 54 \;\; = \;\; 432$
$16 \times 54 = 864$
$\qquad\quad = 1512$

Big numbers multiplication

Practice

Look at the number of items in each box. Calculate how many items you have altogether when you buy more than one box. Work out the answers in your head.

There are 36 scissors per box.
I buy 2 boxes.
2 × 36 = 72 scissors

1 Buy
- a 7
- b 4
- c 5
- d 3
- e 6

36 scissors per box

2 Buy
- a 8
- b 4
- c 9
- d 3
- e 5

48 glue sticks per box

3 Buy
- a 5
- b 3
- c 7
- d 6
- e 9

27 calculators per box

4 Buy
- a 8
- b 5
- c 3
- d 7
- e 6

24 rubbers per box

5 Buy
- a 4
- b 8
- c 3
- d 7
- e 6

38 paint bottles per box

6 Buy
- a 9
- b 5
- c 6
- d 4
- e 8

54 paperclips per box

7 Buy
- a 3
- b 8
- c 5
- d 6
- e 2

63 sharpeners per box

8 Buy
- a 7
- b 4
- c 3
- d 5
- e 8

45 pencils per box

Refresher

Example

$32 \times 3 = (30 \times 3) + (2 \times 3)$

$= 90 \quad\quad + 6$

$= 96$

Partition each of these calculations to find the answer.

a $47 \times 3 =$ b $44 \times 6 =$ c $76 \times 8 =$ d 36×9 e 53×8

f 78×6 g 65×4 h 48×7 i 93×4 j 86×5

Challenge

Missing number game

You need:
- Set of number cards 10–100
- 0–9 die

What to do

Play with a partner

1 Place the number cards face down in a pile. Take turns to turn the top card over.

2 Take turns to roll the die in secret. Multiply the number on the die by the number on the card. Write the answer.

3 The other player works out which number was thrown on the die.

Here are the results of a game played by two children.
Work out which number was rolled on the die each time.

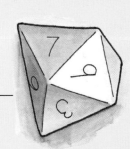

	Jack			Sam	
a	64 ×	= 384	37 ×		= 148
b	45 ×	= 135	56 ×		= 392
c	59 ×	= 236	65 ×		= 585
d	73 ×	= 511	83 ×		= 415
e	87 ×	= 696	78 ×		= 234
f	68 ×	= 612	49 ×		= 392
g	96 ×	= 480	74 ×		= 444

Grid multiplication

Practice

Set out each of the following calculations using the grid method.

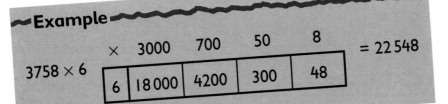

Example

×	3000	700	50	8
6	18 000	4200	300	48

3758×6 = 22 548

1 a $3626 \times 5 = $ 　

b $6324 \times 3 = $ 　

c $2761 \times 4 = $ 　

d $8192 \times 9 = $ 　

e $5293 \times 8 = $ 　

f $1423 \times 3 = $ 　

g $5732 \times 5 = $ 　

h $4901 \times 4 = $ 　

i $6882 \times 9 = $ 　

j $9123 \times 4 = $ 　

k $6812 \times 3 = $ 　

l $8002 \times 5 = $ 　

m $4375 \times 6 = $ 　

n $8534 \times 7 = $ 　

o $2964 \times 6 = $ 　

2 a $1287 \times 7 = $ 　

b $4032 \times 2 = $ 　

c $3504 \times 6 = $ 　

d $7123 \times 5 = $ 　

e $3875 \times 6 = $ 　

f $2081 \times 7 = $ 　

g $8160 \times 8 = $ 　

h $7214 \times 2 = $ 　

i $4190 \times 8 = $ 　

j $2102 \times 6 = $ 　

k $7575 \times 7 = $ 　

l $3761 \times 9 = $ 　

m $3052 \times 3 = $ 　

n $1359 \times 4 = $ 　

o $2658 \times 4 = $

Refresher

1 Set out each of the following calculations using the grid method.

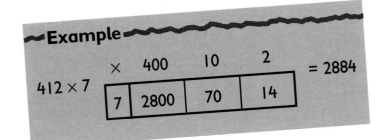

Example

412×7

×	400	10	2
7	2800	70	14

= 2884

a $326 \times 8 =$ ☐

b $124 \times 6 =$ ☐

c $641 \times 7 =$ ☐

d $532 \times 4 =$ ☐

e $375 \times 3 =$ ☐

f $287 \times 9 =$ ☐

g $704 \times 3 =$ ☐

h $642 \times 5 =$ ☐

i $493 \times 8 =$ ☐

Challenge

1 For each question use the grid method to work out the missing digit.

Example

$4\_28 \times 5$

×	4000	100	20	8
5	20 000	500	100	40

= 20 640

a $7\_24 \times 3$ ×☐☐☐☐ = 21 372

b $458\_ \times 7$ ×☐☐☐☐ = 32 081

c $34\_6 \times 6$ ×☐☐☐☐ = 20 556

d $\_679 \times 9$ ×☐☐☐☐ = 15 111

e $25\_8 \times 8$ ×☐☐☐☐ = 20 304

f $5\_03 \times 5$ ×☐☐☐☐ = 25 515

g $924\_ \times 2$ ×☐☐☐☐ = 18 490

h $6\_10 \times 3$ ×☐☐☐☐ = 19 230

Multiplication methods

Practice

Example

$3892 \times 4 \approx 4000 \times 4 = 1600$

		3	8	9	2
$\times$					4
(3000×4)	1	2	0	0	0
(800×4)		3	2	0	0
(90×4)			3	6	0
(2×4)					8
	1	5	5	6	8

Approximate your answer first. Use the standard method to record your working.

a 4172×5

b 3652×3

c 2936×4

d 3845×5

e 2463×4

f 5637×6

g 5418×7

h 6247×6

i 7246×8

j 6843×7

k 7476×9

l 6947×8

Remember

Keep the numbers in the correct columns!

Refresher

Look at the instruction and write multiplication facts for each bag of numbers.

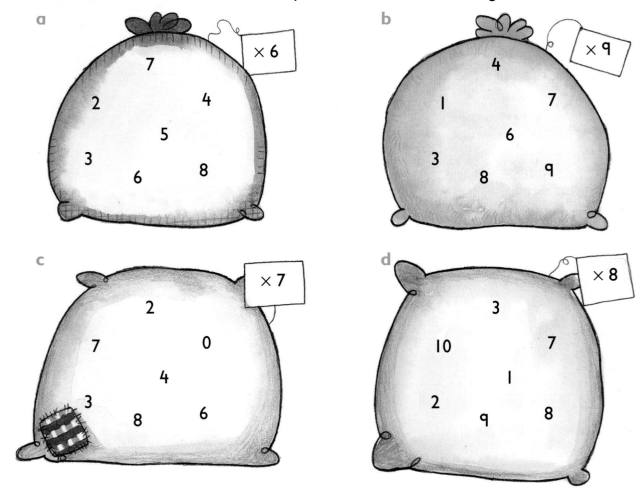

a × 6

7 2 4 5 3 6 8

b × 9

4 1 7 6 3 8 9

c × 7

2 7 0 4 3 8 6

d × 8

3 10 7 1 2 9 8

Challenge

Copy the grid. Fill in the answers on the grid by multiplying the numbers in each horizontal line by 5 and each vertical line by 3.

(Some answers can be done mentally. Use a standard method to find the other answers.)

	21				
×3	7	35			

× 5

Mailbag multiplication

Practice

1 For each of the calculations in the Refresher Activity, work out the answer using the standard method of recording.

2 Calculate the answers to these problems. Approximate the answer first, then use the standard method of recording.

a

The local post office sold 4867 first class stamps each day for 5 days. What was the total number of stamps sold?

b

There are 6 collections a day from the post box. 3956 letters are collected each time. How many letters are collected in a day?

c

The postman delivers on average 4328 letters in the first delivery and 2674 letters in the second delivery each day for the week (6 days). How many letters in both deliveries over the week?

d

An average of 3265 second class stamps were sold on each of the first 3 days of the week. 5632 were sold on each of the following 3 days. What was the total number sold?

e

2437 vans are used each day to collect mail. How many trips are made by the vans over a 5-day period?

f

The average number of letters posted to Spain in a week from one city was 2658. How many letters would be sent to Spain over a 6-week period?

Refresher

Approximate the answer to each calculation.

a $1873 \times 4 \approx$

b $2736 \times 5 \approx$

c $2432 \times 4 \approx$

d $3347 \times 3 \approx$

e $4759 \times 5 \approx$

f $2653 \times 6 \approx$

g $3748 \times 9 \approx$

h $4592 \times 8 \approx$

i $2963 \times 7 \approx$

j $3264 \times 6 \approx$

k $5643 \times 7 \approx$

l $4976 \times 8 \approx$

m $6475 \times 6 \approx$

n $5847 \times 4 \approx$

o $4346 \times 8 \approx$

Challenge

1 Five answers total 9996.
   Can you find them?

4998×2

3742×3

1666×6

3274×5

3332×3

2499×4

1428×7

2749×4

2 Five answers total 15 060.
   Can you find them?

5020×3

3012×5

2955×4

2510×6

2410×7

3765×4

6325×2

7530×2

Decimal decisions

Practice

The machines partition numbers into whole numbers and decimal numbers. Write each number as it will come out of the machine.

Example
$4·6 = (4·0 + 0·6)$
$13·6 = (10·0 + 3·0 + 0·6)$

1

a 6·3

b 7·2

c 3·5

d 4·8

e 8·9

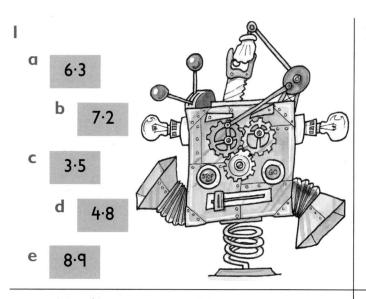

2

a 24·6

b 18·3

c 6·42

d 7·78

e 3·59

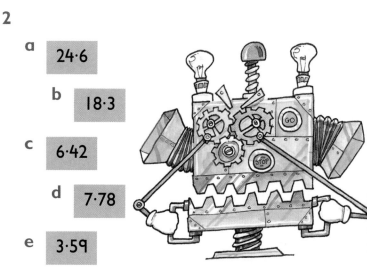

3

a 4·82

b 9·3

c 15·4

d 7·03

e 2·9

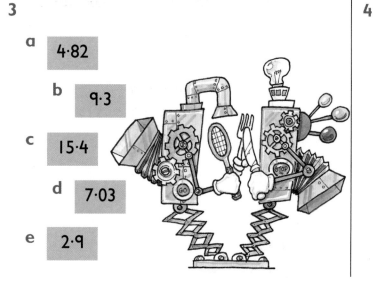

4

a 12·6

b 9·92

c 4·35

d 26·1

e 8·09

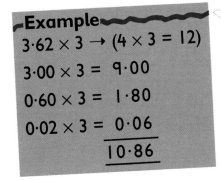

5

You need:
● 0–9 die

For each of the numbers above, roll the die to give you the number to multiply by. Approximate first, then work out the calculations using the standard method of multiplying decimals.

Example
$3·62 × 3 → (4 × 3 = 12)$
$3·00 × 3 = 9·00$
$0·60 × 3 = 1·80$
$0·02 × 3 = 0·06$
―――――
$10·86$

Refresher

Write the whole number each decimal number is between.
Now circle the whole number the decimal number is closest to.
The first one is done for you.

1 a **4** ← 4·6 → (**5**)   2 a ☐ ←3·67→ ☐   3 a ☐ ←16·1→ ☐

 b ☐ ← 3·4 → ☐   b ☐ ←4·82→ ☐   b ☐ ←7·06→ ☐

 c ☐ ← 7·8 → ☐   c ☐ ←8·46→ ☐   c ☐ ←14·92→ ☐

 d ☐ ←25·9→ ☐   d ☐ ←9·35→ ☐   d ☐ ←31·7→ ☐

 e ☐ ←12·1→ ☐   e ☐ ←5·02→ ☐   e ☐ ←48·3→ ☐

Challenge

1 For each set of calculations, decide which gives the largest answer by approximating.
   Write your approximations.

a   7·8 × 4   b   7·05 × 6   c   13·2 × 6
    8·4 × 7   6·70 × 5   12·6 × 3
    4·8 × 7   5·60 × 7   16·3 × 2
    4·7 × 8   6·50 × 7   12·3 × 6

d   8·45 × 3   e   4·62 × 3
    5·43 × 8   5·42 × 3
    5·83 × 4   5·32 × 4
    8·34 × 5   3·42 × 6

2 Find the difference between the actual answers to the largest and
   smallest calculations in each set.

Musical problems

Practice

Read the word problems, then choose an appropriate method of calculating your answer: mental, mental with jottings or paper and pencil.

a The Music Store has 7 stereo systems in stock. What is the total value?

b How much money would you save buying 8 cassettes instead of 8 CDs?

c The Music Store has 3876 cassettes in stock. What is the total value? If half of the total value is profit to the shop, how much money do they make?

d The manager of the Music Store compiles a list of orders. The order consists of 16 Walkmans, 15 clock radios, 7 tape recorders and 8 CD racks. If all of these items are sold, how much money will be taken by the store?

e Mum and Dad buy Joshua 6 CDs for his Christmas present. What is the total cost? How much change do they get from £50?

f A music magazine is published monthly. Jasmine takes out a year's subscription to the magazine. How much does she spend?

Refresher

Look at the items in the Music Store on the opposite page.
For each word problem, decide which operation you will
use to answer the question. Work the answer out in your head.
Record the calculation.

a Buy 8 walkmans. What is the total cost?

b The shop sells 16 clock radios. How much money do they make?

c Buy 36 cassettes in a year. How much money do you spend?

d The CD rack holds 25 CDs. You have £200. Approximate whether you have enough money to fill the rack.

e Jamie buys 12 clock radios. Julie buys 18 walkmans. How much more does Julie spend?

f How many sets of headphones can you buy with £100?

g Buy 1 tape recorder, a set of headphones and 3 cassettes. How much do you spend?

h Buy 2 stereo systems, and 4 clock radios. What is the total cost?

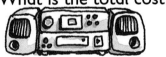

i Buy 6 magazines. You have £20. Do you have enough money?

Challenge

Longdale School has £10 000 to spend on music items.

1 Work out what they can buy and in what quantities.

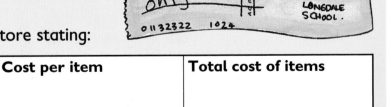

2 Prepare an invoice from the Music Store stating:

Items	Number of items	Cost per item	Total cost of items

3 How much change from £10 000 does the school receive?

Improper and proper fractions

Practice

1 Use the diagrams to help you change the improper fractions to mixed numbers and the mixed numbers to improper fractions.

a $\frac{7}{4}$ 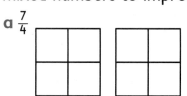 b $\frac{9}{5}$ 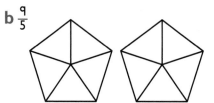 c $\frac{12}{7}$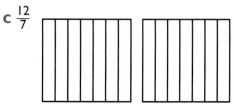

d $1\frac{2}{6}$ 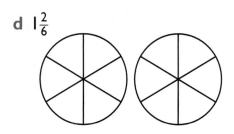 e $1\frac{3}{7}$ 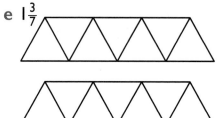 f $1\frac{4}{10}$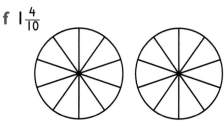

2 Change these improper fractions to mixed numbers.

a $\frac{15}{8}$ b $\frac{4}{3}$ c $\frac{9}{8}$ d $\frac{13}{6}$ e $\frac{17}{4}$

f $\frac{11}{2}$ g $\frac{16}{5}$ h $\frac{20}{9}$ i $\frac{18}{10}$ j $\frac{121}{100}$

3 Change these mixed numbers to improper fractions.

a $1\frac{3}{6}$ b $1\frac{4}{5}$ c $1\frac{2}{7}$ d $2\frac{4}{8}$ e $2\frac{1}{3}$

f $2\frac{6}{10}$ g $2\frac{8}{9}$ h $2\frac{7}{12}$ i $3\frac{3}{10}$ j $3\frac{18}{100}$

I'm a proper fraction.

I'm an improper fraction.

30

Refresher

$$\frac{1}{2} = \frac{\text{numerator}}{\text{denominator}}$$

Example

$\frac{7}{5}$ 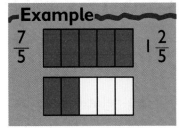 $1\frac{2}{5}$

1 Change these improper fractions to mixed numbers.
   Use the diagrams to help you.

a $\frac{4}{3}$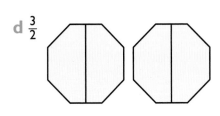

b $\frac{8}{6}$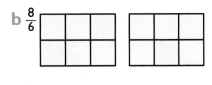

c $\frac{7}{4}$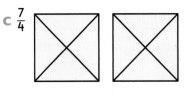

d $\frac{3}{2}$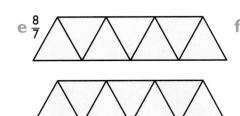

e $\frac{8}{7}$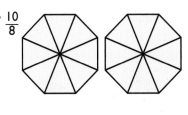

f $\frac{10}{8}$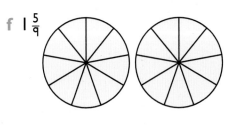

2 Change these mixed numbers to improper fractions.
   Use the diagrams to help you.

a $1\frac{2}{6}$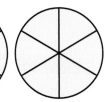

b $1\frac{3}{5}$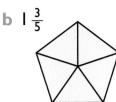

c $1\frac{5}{7}$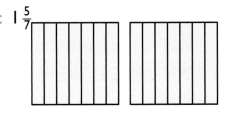

d $1\frac{9}{10}$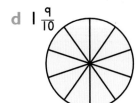

e $1\frac{3}{4}$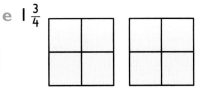

f $1\frac{5}{9}$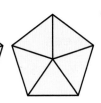

Challenge

Look back at your answers in the Practice section.

a Put the mixed numbers from question 2 in order.

b Put the improper fractions from question 3 in order.

Fraction relations

Practice

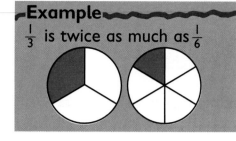
1 What is the relationship between these fractions?
Use the diagrams to help you.

a $\frac{1}{2}, \frac{1}{6}$

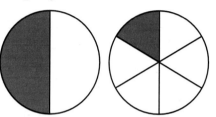

b $\frac{1}{2}, \frac{1}{8}$

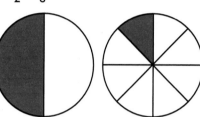

c $\frac{1}{2}, \frac{1}{10}$

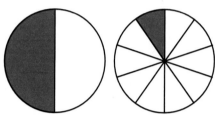

d $\frac{1}{2}, \frac{1}{12}$

e $\frac{1}{2}, \frac{1}{14}$

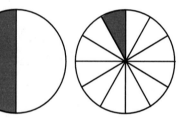
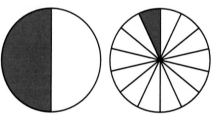

2 Work out the relationship between
these fractions by using division.

a $\frac{1}{4}, \frac{1}{16}$

b $\frac{1}{4}, \frac{1}{12}$

c $\frac{1}{4}, \frac{1}{20}$

d $\frac{1}{10}, \frac{1}{100}$

e $\frac{1}{10}, \frac{1}{30}$

f $\frac{1}{10}, \frac{1}{40}$

g $\frac{1}{5}, \frac{1}{15}$

h $\frac{1}{5}, \frac{1}{100}$

Example
$\frac{1}{3}, \frac{1}{6}$
$6 \div 3 = 2$
So $\frac{1}{3}$ is 2 times as big as $\frac{1}{6}$

Example

$\frac{1}{3}$ is 3 times as big as $\frac{1}{9}$

Refresher

What is the relationship between these fractions?
Use the diagrams to help you.

a $\frac{1}{2}, \frac{1}{4}$

b $\frac{1}{4}, \frac{1}{8}$

c $\frac{1}{3}, \frac{1}{6}$

d $\frac{1}{5}, \frac{1}{10}$

e $\frac{1}{6}, \frac{1}{12}$

f $\frac{1}{10}, \frac{1}{20}$

g $\frac{1}{7}, \frac{1}{14}$

h $\frac{1}{8}, \frac{1}{16}$

Challenge

Explain in writing how to work out the relationship between fractions using division.

Getting simpler

Practice

1 Reduce the fractions to their simplest form.

a $\frac{3}{9}$ b $\frac{4}{12}$ c $\frac{6}{18}$ d $\frac{10}{30}$

e $\frac{8}{16}$ f $\frac{7}{21}$ g $\frac{6}{16}$ h $\frac{8}{12}$

i $\frac{9}{15}$ j $\frac{25}{100}$ k $\frac{30}{100}$ l $\frac{45}{100}$

m $\frac{18}{24}$ n $\frac{14}{36}$ o $\frac{80}{100}$ p $\frac{21}{49}$

2 Multiply the numerator and denominator by 2 to find an equivalent fraction.

a $\frac{3}{5}$ b $\frac{4}{7}$ c $\frac{5}{9}$ d $\frac{3}{7}$

e $\frac{1}{4}$ f $\frac{3}{10}$ g $\frac{2}{6}$ h $\frac{5}{8}$

i $\frac{4}{5}$ j $\frac{2}{9}$ k $\frac{3}{4}$ l $\frac{2}{8}$

m $\frac{5}{6}$ n $\frac{4}{5}$ o $\frac{5}{7}$ p $\frac{3}{9}$

Refresher

1 Divide the numerator and the denominator by 2 to simplify the fractions.

a $\dfrac{2}{4} = \dfrac{\square}{\square}$

b $\dfrac{4}{8} = \dfrac{\square}{\square}$

c $\dfrac{4}{12} = \dfrac{\square}{\square}$

d $\dfrac{2}{6} = \dfrac{\square}{\square}$

e $\dfrac{2}{8} = \dfrac{\square}{\square}$

f $\dfrac{4}{16} = \dfrac{\square}{\square}$

g $\dfrac{6}{8} = \dfrac{\square}{\square}$

h $\dfrac{6}{12} = \dfrac{\square}{\square}$

i $\dfrac{6}{18} = \dfrac{\square}{\square}$

j $\dfrac{8}{12} = \dfrac{\square}{\square}$

2 Divide the numerator and the denominator by 3 to simplify the fractions.

a $\dfrac{3}{6}$

b $\dfrac{6}{12}$

c $\dfrac{3}{9}$

d $\dfrac{6}{9}$

e $\dfrac{3}{12}$

f $\dfrac{6}{18}$

g $\dfrac{9}{12}$

h $\dfrac{12}{18}$

i $\dfrac{9}{15}$

j $\dfrac{6}{15}$

Challenge

Look at the fractions in question 2 of the Practice Activity. Multiply the numerators and denominators by other numbers to find other equivalent fractions.

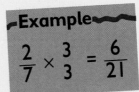

35

- Know what each digit represents in a number with up to three decimal places
- Give a decimal fraction lying between two others

Decimal fractions

Practice

1 Read these decimal fractions. What does the red digit represent?

a 6·872 b 5·314 c 3·129

d 2·004 e 8·068 f 1·507

2 Order each group of decimal fractions from smallest to largest.

a 4·687, 4·293, 4·106, 4·005, 4·972

b 3·612, 5·892, 4·637, 2·637, 1·073

c 0·832, 0·045, 1·405, 2·832, 1·504

d 5·310, 4·624, 5·130, 0·513, 0·462

e 6·723, 6·581, 6·729, 6·735, 6·526

3 Draw a number line and write the thousandths that come between these hundredths.

Example

Between 1·24 and 1·25

1·24 1·241 1·242 1·243 1·244 ......

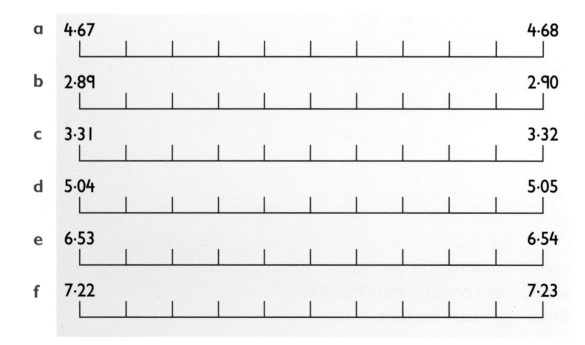

a 4·67 ... 4·68

b 2·89 ... 2·90

c 3·31 ... 3·32

d 5·04 ... 5·05

e 6·53 ... 6·54

f 7·22 ... 7·23

Refresher

1 Read these decimal fractions. What does the red digit represent?

　a 2·56　　　b 3·58　　　c 1·09　　　d 7·67　　　e 4·84

2 Order each group of decimal fractions from smallest to largest.

　a 5·62, 4·89, 3·72, 1·63, 2·04　　　b 4·86, 4·93, 4·12, 4·51, 4·66

　c 0·72, 0·78, 0·75, 0·79, 0·74　　　d 1·51, 1·82, 1·55, 1·87, 1·59

　e 4·21, 2·41, 4·12, 2·14, 2·22

3 Draw a number line and write the hundredths that come between these tenths.

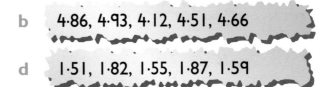

Example

Between 1·6 and 1·7

1·6　1·61　1·62　1·63　1·64　1·65　1·66

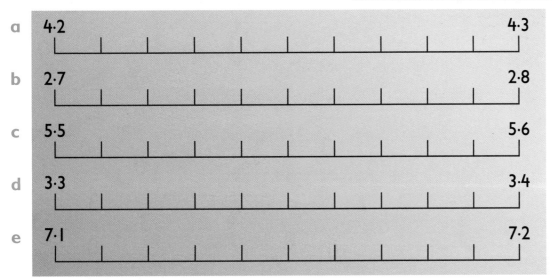

a 4·2 .... 4·3

b 2·7 .... 2·8

c 5·5 .... 5·6

d 3·3 .... 3·4

e 7·1 .... 7·2

Challenge

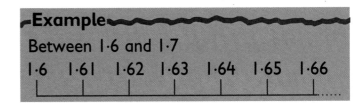

Example
8 · 6 2 5

1 Using the digits on the cards, how many different numbers to 3 decimal places can you make? You must use all the digits each time.

5　8　6　2

2 Explain how you know that you have found all the possible numbers.

3 Now order the numbers from smallest to largest.

Fraction and decimal clouds

Practice

Use the digits in the clouds to make a fraction and its decimal equivalent.

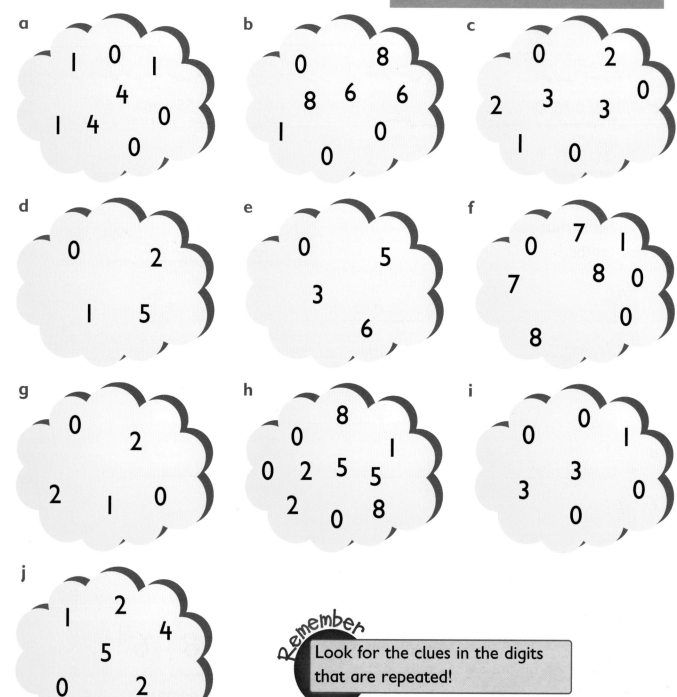

a

b

c

d

e

f

g

h

i

j

Remember

Look for the clues in the digits that are repeated!

Refresher

Use the digits in the stars to make
a fraction and its decimal equivalent.

a

b

c

d

e

f

g

h

i

Challenge

Choose the decimal that is equal to the fraction.

a $\dfrac{193}{100}$ 1·93   0·193   10·193   19·13

b $\dfrac{47}{1000}$ 0·47   47·00   0·047   4·07

c $\dfrac{2}{1000}$ 0·02   0·2   0·002   0·0002

d $\dfrac{673}{1000}$ 0·763   0·673   6·73   0·0673

e $\dfrac{405}{1000}$ 0·045   0·504   4·405   0·405   0·004

Decimal measures

Practice

1 What is the decimal relationship between each of these two units?
Think how many of one there are in the other.

   a   kilograms and grams

   b   metres and centimetres

   c   litres and millilitres

   d   kilometres and metres

   e   centimetres and millimetres

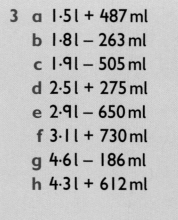

> There are 1000 grams in a kilogram. So 1 gram is 0.001 kg

Work out these calculations. You will need to change one of the measures.

2 a 4 m + 50 cm
   b 7 km − 20 m
   c 2·5 km + 346 m
   d 3·1 cm + 10 mm
   e 2·8 m − 64 cm
   f 3·7 km − 452 m
   g 4·3 cm + 25 mm
   h 1·9 km − 380 m
   i 3·2 km + 672 m
   j 4·5 m − 28 cm

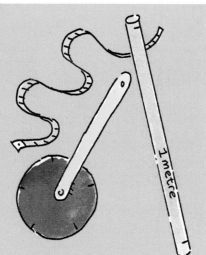
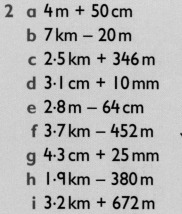

3 a 1·5 l + 487 ml
   b 1·8 l − 263 ml
   c 1·9 l − 505 ml
   d 2·5 l + 275 ml
   e 2·9 l − 650 ml
   f 3·1 l + 730 ml
   g 4·6 l − 186 ml
   h 4·3 l + 612 ml

4 a 2·8 kg − 265 g
   b 3·7 kg − 315 g
   c 4·1 kg + 485 g
   d 5·6 kg + 246 g
   e 4·8 kg − 571 g
   f 6·2 kg + 354 g
   g 7·6 kg − 287 g
   h 8·5 kg + 300 g

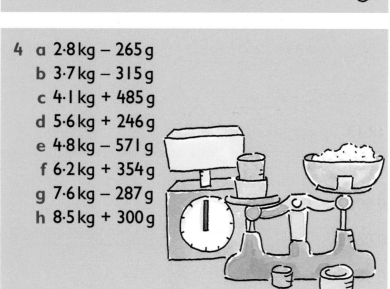

Refresher

Work out the calculations. Use the illustration to help you.

1 a 1·2 l + 300 ml
   b 1·5 l + 250 ml
   c 1·3 l + 600 ml
   d 1·2 l + 340 ml
   e 1·4 l + 265 ml
   f 1·6 l + 315 ml
   g 1·1 l + 548 ml
   h 1·7 l + 247 ml
   i 1·5 l + 324 ml
   j 1·3 l + 653 ml

2 a 1·8 l − 200 ml
   b 1·7 l − 350 ml
   c 1·9 l − 460 ml
   d 1·7 l − 152 ml
   e 1·6 l − 210 ml
   f 1·8 l − 328 ml
   g 1·7 l − 239 ml
   h 1·4 l − 172 ml
   i 1·6 l − 584 ml
   j 1·2 l − 105 ml

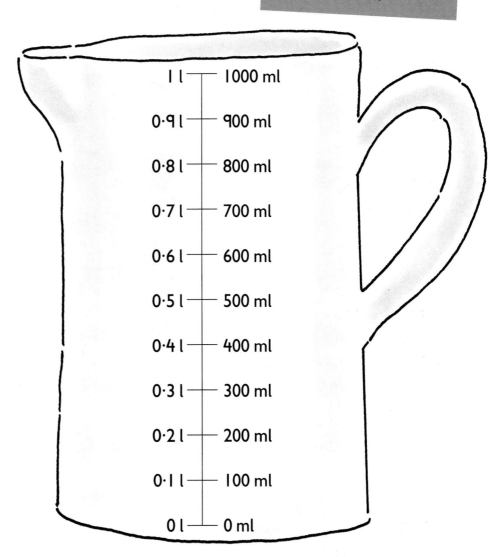

Challenge

Convert these measures.

a 750 grams to kilograms
b 45 millimetres to centimetres
c 567 metres to kilometres
d 854 grams to kilograms
e 203 metres to kilometres
f 1254 grams to kilograms
g 1763 metres to kilometres
h 1965 millilitres to litres
i 2763 grams to kilograms
j 2653 metres to kilometres

Percentage and fraction prices

Practice

1 Look at the labels on the clothes and answer the questions.

T-shirt

Cotton 80%
Polyamide 10%
Lycra 10%

jumper

75% wool
25% acrylic

cardigan

12$\frac{1}{2}$% elastane
87·5% acrylic

 a What **fraction** of the T-shirt is cotton? Polyamide? Lycra?
 b What **fraction** of the jumper is wool? Acrylic?
 c What **fraction** of the cardigan is elastane? Acrylic?
 d How much more acrylic is in the cardigan than the jumper?
    First give your answer as a percentage, then as a fraction.

2 Copy these fractions and decimals into your book.
   Circle the ones that are **more** than the fraction in the box.

   a $\frac{1}{2}$ 52%, $\frac{2}{6}$, $\frac{5}{8}$, 45%, 67%

   b $\frac{1}{4}$ 24%, 42%, $\frac{2}{6}$, $\frac{4}{12}$, 27%

   c $\frac{1}{10}$ $\frac{12}{1000}$, 1%, 11%, $\frac{11}{100}$, $\frac{3}{20}$

   d $\frac{1}{3}$ 35%, $\frac{4}{9}$, $\frac{2}{6}$, 31%, $\frac{4}{8}$

   e $\frac{1}{8}$ 12%, $\frac{3}{16}$, 13%, $\frac{1}{10}$, $\frac{1}{4}$

3 Look at an item of your own clothing that is made of more than one
   material. Copy the percentages into your book. Round the numbers
   to the nearest multiple of 10. Convert the percentages to fractions.

4 Now swap with a friend and check that they have converted their
   percentages correctly.

Refresher

1 Write the equivalent fractions for these percentages.
Use the 100 grid to help you. Now write what
fraction of the grid would be shaded.

a 50%   b 25%   c 75%

d 10%   e 20%

2 Look at the labels above the clothes.
On each item of clothing one
percentage has been worn away.
What is the missing percentage?

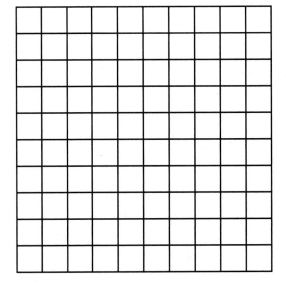

trousers

50% cotton
☐ polyamide

shirt

75% cotton
☐ lycra

jumper

20% acrylic
☐ wool

T-shirt

25% lycra
25% acrylic
☐ cotton

Challenge

Order the fractions and percentages from smallest to largest.

a $\frac{3}{8}$, 13%, 27%, $\frac{2}{8}$, 40%, $\frac{1}{8}$

b $\frac{2}{3}$, 71%, 35%, 22%, 1%, $\frac{1}{3}$

c $\frac{1}{2}$, 86%, $\frac{3}{4}$, 68%, $\frac{3}{8}$, 45%

d $\frac{5}{10}$, 49%, $\frac{1}{10}$, $\frac{8}{10}$, 9%, 74%

e $\frac{3}{6}$, 48%, $\frac{5}{8}$, 51%, $\frac{2}{3}$, 66%

School percentages

Practice

Work out the percentages for these problems.
Write down the calculation you use.

1 There are 24 children in a year 6 class.

   a 25% of them have blue eyes. How many children is this?

   b $12\frac{1}{2}$% of the class are away today. How many children is this?
   What fraction of the class are away?

   c 16 children are girls. What percentage of the class is this?
   What fraction of the class are girls?

   d The teacher estimates that about 10% of the class will forget their
   homework tomorrow. About how many children will this be?

   e 5 children finish their work early. About what percentage of
   the class is this?

2 There are 320 children at Bankside School.

   a 75% of them wear school uniform. How many children is this?

   b 30% of them are in Keystage 1. How many children in Keystage 2?

   c 64 children cycle to school. What percentage of the school is this?

   d About a third of the children do not have any brothers or sisters
   at the school. What percentage of the school is this? About how
   many children is this?

   e 85 children are going out on a trip today. About what percentage
   of the school is this?

Refresher

Work out the percentages to these problems.
Write down the calculation you use.

There are 20 children going on an outing.

a 50% of them are girls. How many children is that?

b 25% of the children have got crisps with their lunch.
How many children is that?

c How many children have not got crisps with their lunch? What
percentage of the children is this?

d 10% of the children have forgotten their spending money. How
many children is this?

e 30% of the children think it will rain later. How many children is
that? What percentage of the children don't think it will rain?
How many children is that?

Challenge

Make up some percentage
questions about your own class.

Remember

If you do not have exact
numbers, use percentages and
fractions that are "about".

Ratio and proportion patterns

Practice

What is the ratio and proportion of these patterns? (First look at how many units there are in each section of the pattern.)

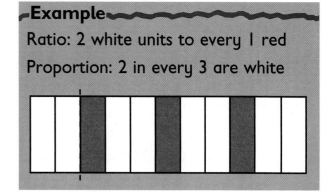
Remember

Use the words:
"to every" for ratio
"in every" for proportion

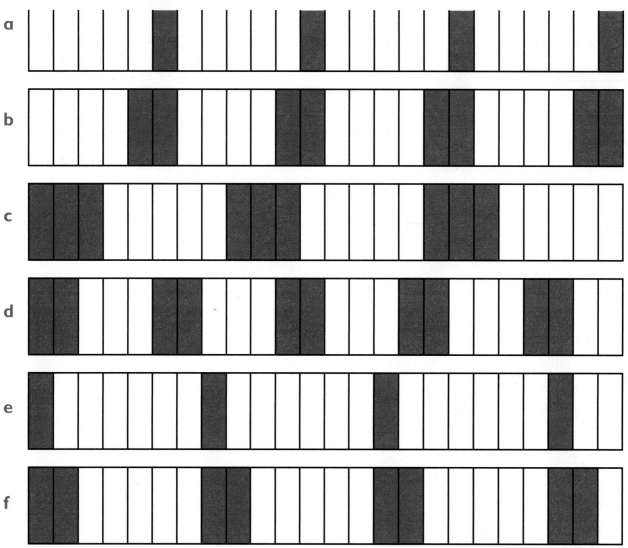

a

b

c

d

e

f

Refresher

Draw one section of each pattern in your book. Then work out the ratio of red to blue squares.

Example

The ratio is 2 blue to every 1 red square

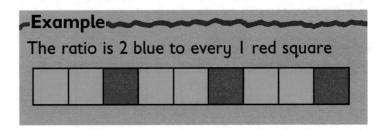

a

The ratio is ☐ red square to every ☐ blue squares.

b

The ratio is ☐ red squares to every ☐ blue squares.

c

The ratio is ☐ red square to every ☐ blue squares.

d

The ratio is ☐ red square to every ☐ blue squares.

e

The ratio is ☐ red squares to every ☐ blue squares.

Challenge

1 Look at the patterns in the Practice section and work out how many squares would be white and how many red if:

   a pattern a went on for 24 squares

   b pattern b went on for 30 squares

   c pattern c went on for 40 squares

   d pattern d went on for 35 squares

   e pattern e went on for 42 squares

   f pattern f went on for 49 squares

2 Explain how you worked out your answers.

Classroom problems

Practice

1 There are 30 children in Y6. For every 2 girls there is 1 boy.

  a What is the ratio of boys to girls?

  b What proportion of the class is boys?

  c How many girls and how many boys are there?

2 The cake recipe says you need 1 egg to make 5 cakes. I want to make 25 cakes.

  a What is the ratio of eggs to cakes?

  b How many eggs will I need?

3 The museum will only allow children to visit if there is a ratio of 1 adult to every 10 children. The school wants to take 50 children.

  a How many adults will need to go on the trip?

  b What is the proportion of adults on the trip?

4 To make orange paint I mixed 2 pots of red to every 4 pots of yellow. Altogether I used 18 pots of paint.

  a What is the ratio of red to yellow paint?

  b What proportion of the paint is red?

  c How many red pots did I use?

  d How many yellow pots did I use?

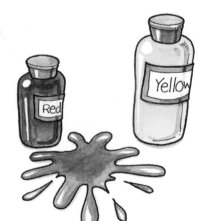

5 When the Y6 class of 32 children were asked if they preferred English or maths homework, the ratio was 3:5. 3 children preferred English to every 5 who preferred maths.

  a How many children preferred English homework?

  b How many preferred maths homework?

  c What proportion of the class preferred English?

  d What proportion of the class preferred maths?

Refresher

1 Lisa has 12 cakes. She gives 1 to Gavin for every 2 she eats herself.

   a What is the ratio of Lisa's cakes to Gavin's?
   b How many cakes will Lisa eat?
   c How many cakes will Gavin eat?

2 John is looking at his football stickers. For every 1 he wants to keep he has 3 he wants to swap.

   a What is the ratio of stickers he wants to keep to those he wants to swap?
   b If he has 16 stickers how many stickers does he want to keep?
   c If he has 24 stickers how many does he want to swap?

3 Ian has counted the flowers in his pots. For every 2 white flowers he has 3 yellow ones. Altogether he has 20 flowers.

   a What is the ratio of white to yellow flowers?
   b How many white flowers are there?
   c How many yellow flowers are there?

Challenge

Write a word problem with:

a a ratio of 2:5

b a ratio of 1:6

c a proportion of 1 in every 3

d a proportion of 2 in every 5

Roll the die probability

Practice

1 Helena rolls an ordinary die once.
What is the probability that she will roll a:

a 2   b 8   c odd number

d 1 or 6   e 2, 3 or 4   f number less than 5

g number more than 0

2 Write the question letters **a** to **g** on this probability scale.

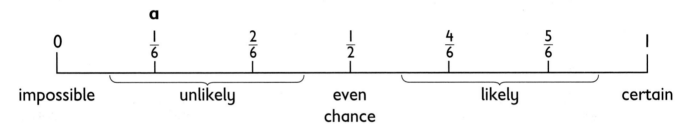

impossible   unlikely   even chance   likely   certain

3 Jamaine spins this spinner once.
What is the probability that the colour she spins will be:

a red   b blue

c any colour   d white

e red or blue   f Which has the greatest chance
                     of happening: red or blue?

4 Write the question letters **a** to **e** on a probability scale.

5 Liam has a special die with these numbers.

He rolls it once. What is the probability that he rolls a:

a 2   b 5   c number less than 4   d 2 or 4

e odd number   f 1   g Which numbers have the same chance of happening?

6 Write the question letters **a** to **f** on a probability scale.

Refresher

1 What is the chance of each of these happening?
Choose your answers from the words on the probability scale.

a You get a 3 with one roll of a 1–6 die.
b You drop a stamp and it falls sticky side up.
c You roll a die and the numbers disappear.
d You flip tails with an ordinary coin.
e You roll an ordinary die once. You get a 2, 3, 4, 5 or 6.
f You flip heads or tails with an ordinary coin.

2 Write the question letters on this probability scale.

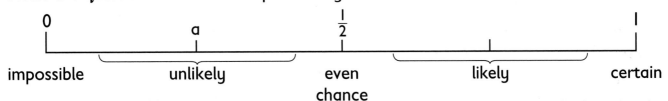

Challenge

Example

What is the probability it is 7?

There is one 7 out of 10 cards.

1 out of 10 = $\frac{1}{10}$ = 0·1.

The probability is 0·1.

1 Daniel shuffles these cards and chooses one without looking.

What is the probability that he will choose a:

a 9   b 11   c an even number   d 1 or 3?

e 7, 8 or 9?   f an odd number   g a number less than 5

h a number above 2 i a number less than 11?

2 Write the question letters a to i on this probability scale.

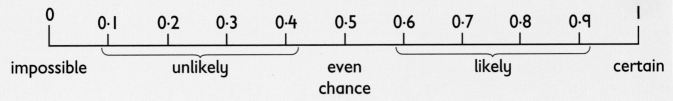

What do you expect?

Practice

Work in pairs. You will need a 1–6 die, squared paper, scissors and crayons.

1 a What is the probability of rolling a 1 or 2 with the die?

   b How many 1s and 2s do you expect in 30 rolls?

   c Take turns to roll the die 30 times. Record the results in a tally chart.

Number rolled	Tally	Total
1 or 2		
3, 4, 5 or 6		

   d Are the results as you expected? Write a sentence.

2 Look at this spinner.

   a Which colour is the spinner most likely to land on?

   b What is the probability it will land on red?

   c Suppose you spin the spinner 40 times.
      How many times do you expect it to land on red?

3 a Follow these instructions to make a spinner.

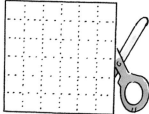 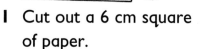 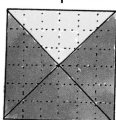 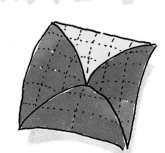

   1 Cut out a 6 cm square   2 Colour it in.   3 Fold opposite corners
      of paper.   to make it spin better

   b Take turns to spin the spinner 40 times.
      Record the results in a tally chart.

Colour	Tally	Total

   c Are the results what you expected? Write a sentence.

Refresher

Work in pairs. You will need a 1–6 die.

1   a   What is the probability of rolling a 6 with the die?
    b   Suppose you roll the die 30 times. How many 6s would you expect?
    c   Decide who will roll the die 30 times. The other person
        records the results in a tally chart.

Number	Tally	Total
6		
1, 2, 3, 4, or 5		

   d   Are the results what you expected? Write a sentence.
2   a   Suppose you rolled the die 60 times. How many 6s would you expect?
    b   Roll the die 30 more times.
    c   Combine your results in a single table.
    d   Are the results as you expected? Write another sentence.

Challenge

Work in pairs. You will need a 0–9 die.

1   a   What is the probability of rolling 7, 8 or 9 with the die?
    b   How many 7s, 8s and 9s would you expect in 30 rolls?
    c   One person rolls the die 30 times. The other person
        records the results in a tally chart.

Number	Tally	Total
7, 8, 9		
0, 1, 2, 3, 4, 5, 6		

   d   Are the results as you expected? Write a sentence.
2   a   Suppose you rolled the die 60 times. How many 7s, 8s and 9s would you expect?
    b   Roll the die 30 more times.
    c   Combine your results into a single table.
    d   Are the results as you expected? Write another sentence.

Television bar charts

Practice

You need:
● squared paper

Akemi timed 35 TV adverts. Here are their lengths, in seconds.

12	24	38	30	17	8	5	22	49	15
11	19	10	15	30	38	18	9	14	18
12	17	29	25	15	36	12	16	7	17
20	25	22	15	7					

1 Copy and complete this tally chart.

Length (seconds)	Tally	Total
1–10		
11–20		

2 Copy and complete this bar chart.

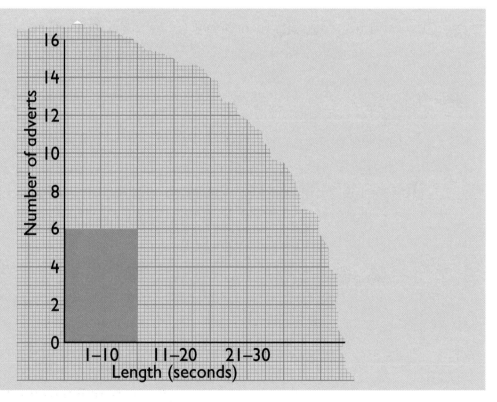

3 a How many TV adverts lasted between 21 and 30 seconds?

   b How many TV adverts lasted more than 30 seconds?

   c Which class contains the most TV programmes?

   d How many adverts lasted less than 21 seconds?

Refresher

The table shows the lengths of children's TV programmes.

Length (minutes)	Number of programmes
1–10	11
11–20	5
21–30	9
31–40	6
41–50	3

You need:
● squared paper

1 a How many programmes lasted between 31 and 40 minutes?
  b Which class has the most programmes?
  c Which class has the least number of programmes?
  d How many programmes lasted longer than 40 minutes?

2 Copy and complete this bar chart.

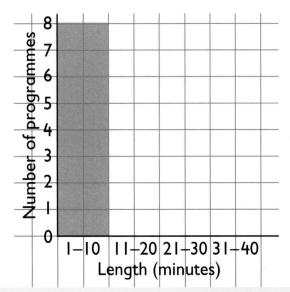

Challenge

TV viewers were asked to rate a programme from 1 to 25. The table shows the results.

Rating	Number of viewers
1–5	9
6–10	32
11–15	57
16–20	75
21–25	41

You need:
● graph paper

1 Copy and complete the bar chart.

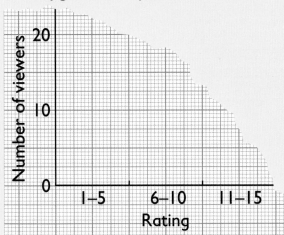

2 Which class contains the most viewers?
3 How many viewers rated the programme above 15?
4 How many more viewers rated the programme from 16–20, than 6–10?
5 How many viewers rated the programme from 6–20?
6 How many viewers are there altogether?

55

Computer racing bar charts

Practice

Claire has a new computer racing game. The bar chart shows the scores she got the first week she played.

Score	Number of games
1–5	
6–10	
11–15	
16–20	
21–25	
26–30	

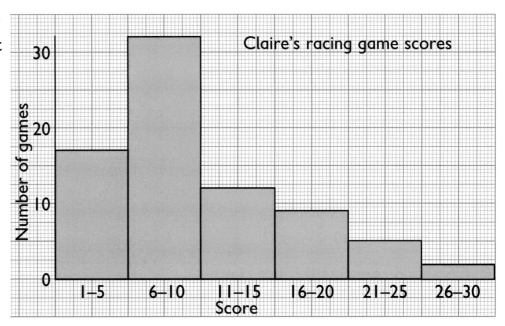

Claire's racing game scores

1 a In how many games was her score from 6 to 10?
  b What was the highest score she could have got?
  c Which class has the most games recorded?
  d In how many games did she score 10 or less?
  e In how many games did she score 16 or more?

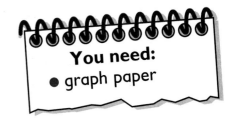

You need:
● graph paper

2 Copy and complete the grouped frequency table.

Claire practised for a few weeks. Then she recorded these scores.

Score	Number of games
1–5	0
6–10	4
11–15	5
16–20	11
21–25	41
26–30	14

3 Draw a new bar chart.

4 a In which class are most games recorded?
  b What was the lowest score she could have got?
  c In how many games did she score between 6 and 15?
  d In how many games did she score between 16 and 25?
  e Do you think Claire has improved? Explain your answer.

Refresher

In a car race, players tried to complete as many laps as possible without crashing. The frequency table shows their results.

Laps	Number of players
1–5	11
6–10	19
11–15	12
16–20	7
21–25	1

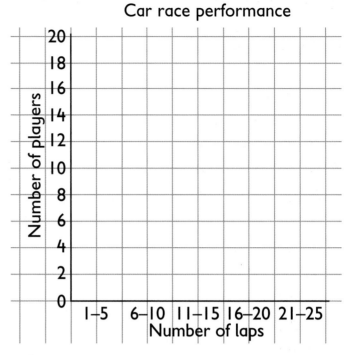

Car race performance

1 Look at the frequency table and draw the bar chart.

2 a How many players crashed within 11 to 15 laps?
  b How many players crashed after less than 6 laps?
  c Which class has the tallest bar?
  d How many players are in this class?
  e What does the shortest bar tell you?

You need:
● squared paper

Challenge

The bar chart shows 100 players' lap times in a computer racing game.

1 a What was the fastest possible time?
  b How many players completed a lap within 31 seconds?
  c How many players took longer than 60 seconds to complete a lap?
  d What does the tallest bar show?
  e Estimate the number of players who did a lap in less than 35 seconds.

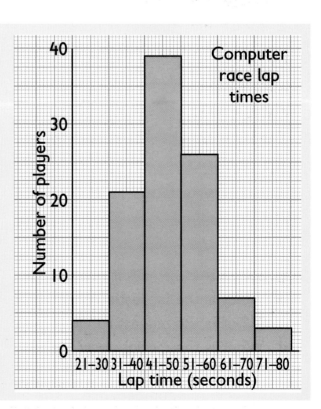

Computer race lap times

Rolling modes and ranges

Practice

Work in groups. You will need two dice and squared paper.

1 a Take turns to roll a die.
  b Write the numbers in a row.
  c Say the mode and range when you add your numbers to the row.
  d Stop when there are 10 numbers in the row.

2 Repeat question 1. This time, use two dice to make two-digit numbers. Say the range only.

3 Copy and complete this tally chart for the group.

Number	Tally	Frequency
11–20		
21–30		

4 a Take turns to roll both dice.
  b Make a two-digit number.
  c Record it in the tally chart.
  d Look at the dice. Which numbers do you think will happen the most?
  e Stop when one set of numbers has about 20 tally marks.

5 Copy and complete the bar chart.

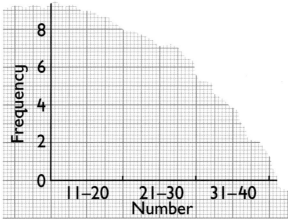

6 a What is the smallest number you could make?
  b What is the largest number you could make?
  c What is the biggest range there could be?
  d What is the modal class?
  e Is this what you predicted?
  f How many numbers are in the modal class?

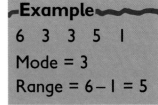

Example
6 3 3 5 1
Mode = 3
Range = 6 – 1 = 5

Example
42 16 55 13
Range = 55 – 13 = 42

58

Refresher

You need:
● a 1–6 die

1 Calculate the mode of these numbers.

  a 3, 7, 7
  b 1, 2, 2, 3, 5, 6
  c 6, 6, 6, 8, 8, 9
  d 2, 9, 9, 10, 10
  e 5, 9, 7, 5, 8, 7, 5
  f 100, 800, 100, 800, 100
  g 7, 2, 1, 9, 7, 2, 3, 8
  h 3, 3, 4, 4, 5, 5, 5, 6, 7, 7, 7, 7, 8, 9, 9, 9, 10

2 Calculate the range of the numbers in question 1.

3 a Roll your die and write the numbers in a row.
  b For each roll, find the mode.
  c Stop when the mode is 1 or 6.
  d Make another row of numbers.

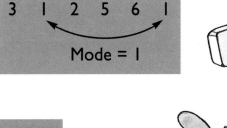

Example

3 1 2 5 6 1

Mode = 1

4 Repeat question 3. This time, stop when the range is 5.

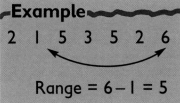

Example

2 1 5 3 5 2 6

Range = 6 – 1 = 5

Challenge

Choose numbers from the grid below to answer these questions. You can repeat the same number.

  a Find three numbers whose mode is 6.
  b Find three numbers whose range is 3.
  c Find three numbers whose mode is 6 and range is 3.
  d Find four numbers whose mode is 20.
  e Find four numbers whose range is 10.
  f Find four numbers whose mode is 20 and range is 10.
  g Find five numbers whose mode is 99.
  h Find five numbers whose range is 1.
  i Find five numbers whose modes are 11 and 19.

Example

Find three numbers whose mode is 11 and whose range is 9.

11, 11, 20

2	21	7	100
20	99	31	60
63	11	9	19
30	6	52	8

Mostly medians

Practice

You need:
● a calculator

Example

3	7	8	11	12	13	15
smallest		median = 11				largest

1 Find the median of these numbers.
Order them first, from smallest to largest.

   a   5, 9, 3, 6, 4   b 2, 8, 2, 8, 2, 8, 2

   c   4, 4, 9, 9, 4, 4, 9, 9, 4   d 50, 30, 10, 30, 20

   e   18, 34, 20, 28, 69, 42, 38   f 2, 6, 3, 3, 2, 1, 7, 4, 9, 1, 4

   g   80, 45, 50, 35, 40, 75, 70, 80, 45   h 3, 9, 1, 1, 3, 9, 1, 1, 3, 3, 9, 1, 3

2 Find the median of these values. Order them first, then find
the middle two numbers. The median is halfway between them.

   a   9, 3, 2, 5   b 6, 2, 2, 6, 2, 6

   c   12, 2, 5, 10, 14, 8   d 5, 4, 4, 4

   e   60, 10, 50, 30,   f 700, 200, 300, 100, 500, 400

   g   5, 3, 3, 5, 7, 5   h 2, 8, 5, 1, 3, 7, 9, 6

3 Find the median of these values.

   a   249, 583, 729, 419, 700   b 3000, 600, 5000, 900, 2400, 750

   c   964, 835, 694   d 2420, 2950

   e   3200, 5800, 9200, 4600, 7200, 3800, 4900

   f   1023, 3051, 2709, 5308, 9025, 4352, 6951, 3502

   g   15240, 7500, 11224, 16100, 10 000, 9986

4 Find the median of these quantities.

   a   30 g, 64 g, 20 g, 80 g, 240 g

   b   £4, £2·50, £12, £16·50, £11, £5·50, £9

   c   140 cm, 250 cm, 160 cm, 300 cm, 92 cm, 200 cm

   d   £1·29, 75p, £2·43, £1, 98p

   e   7 g, 2 g, 2 g, 9 g, 5 g, 5 g, 11 g, 2 g, 6 g, 8 g, 11 g, 8 g

   f   2500 ml, 600 ml, 1600 ml, 400 ml

   g   £1·99, £4·63, £5·84, £6·20, £6·52, £7·00

Refresher

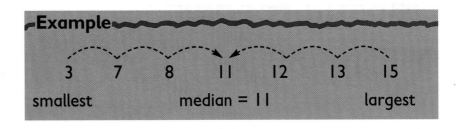

Example

3   7   8   11   12   13   15

smallest   median = 11   largest

1 Find the median (middle number).

   a 2, 5, 9   b 1, 1, 2, 3, 7   c 4, 6, 6, 7, 8   d 2, 2, 2, 6, 6, 6, 6

   e 50, 60, 80, 80 90   f 19, 28, 51   g 7, 32, 59, 71, 99   h 12, 22, 38, 40, 42, 58, 63

2 Find the median (halfway between the middle two numbers).

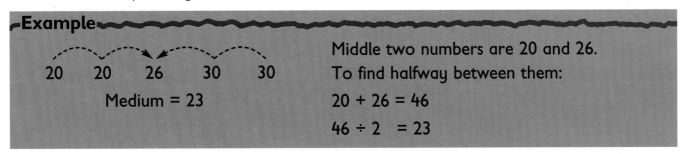

Example

20   20   26   30   30

Medium = 23

Middle two numbers are 20 and 26.
To find halfway between them:

20 + 26 = 46

46 ÷ 2 = 23

   a 5, 7, 9, 10   b 2, 2, 3, 4, 6, 8

   c 0, 0, 0, 4, 4, 5   d 10, 10, 20, 20, 30, 40, 60, 70

   e 1, 1, 2, 3, 3, 4, 5, 5, 6, 8   f 52, 53, 53, 56

   g 300, 300, 400, 450, 500, 700   h 16, 18, 18, 19, 20, 20, 21, 26

3 Find the median of these numbers.

   a 4, 9, 10   b 1, 1, 5, 6   c 2, 2, 4, 9, 10

   d 20, 50, 50, 55, 60, 90   e 0, 0, 5, 9, 14, 23, 27   f 7, 7, 8, 8, 8, 9, 9, 9, 10, 10

Challenge

Sandy counted the crisps in the packets of different brands.

1 Calculate the mode for each brand. Which brand has the highest mode?

31, 35, 39, 30, 40, 38, 36, 30, 37   35, 37, 34, 35, 36, 34, 35, 37   39, 22, 48, 45, 30, 24, 27, 32, 23, 37

2 Calculate the median for each brand. Which brand has the highest median?

3 Calculate the range for each brand. Which brand has the narrowest range?

4 If each brand costs the same, which is the best value? Explain you answer.

Mostly means

Practice

1 Find the mean of these numbers.

   a 4, 14   b 5, 5, 20

   c 3, 3, 7, 7   d 0, 0, 3, 4, 5

   e 10, 10, 10, 20, 20   f 1, 2, 3, 1, 2, 3, 1, 3

   g 1, 4, 1, 4, 1, 4, 6   h 10, 10, 5, 10, 15, 10, 5, 5, 10, 10

2 Find the mean of these weights.

   a 100 g, 400 g   b 1 g, 2 g, 2 g, 5 g, 10 g

   c 100 g, 300 g, 100 g, 300 g   d 10 g, 20 g, 20 g, 40 g, 50 g, 100 g

   e 1 g, 10 g, 5 g, 2 g, 25 g, 2 g, 5 g, 10 g, 21 g

   f 20 g, 45 g, 30 g, 10 g, 15 g, 25 g, 20 g, 15 g, 20 g, 30 g

3 Find the mean of these numbers. Use your calculator.

   a 94, 73   b 48, 60, 72, 38

   c 231, 162, 453   d 7, 17, 27, 37, 47, 57

   e 1250, 4890, 2720, 1990   f 1, 101, 110, 11, 101, 111, 1, 110

   g 9, 17, 28, 39, 46, 58, 71, 93, 104, 129

4 Find the mean of these prices. Use your calculator.

   a £7, £4   b £9, £12, £6, £10

   c £67, £93, £84, £32, £99, £18   d £2·50, £1·75, £3·01

   e £1·20, £7·40, £3·10, £9·20, £6·60, £2, £4·80, £9·70

   f £2, £5, £3, £1, £7, £8·50, £2·50, £1, £1, £10

   g 30p, £1·80, 60p, £3·90, 80p

Refresher

Example
10, 22   Total = 10 + 22 = 32   32 ÷ 2 = 16   Mean = 16

1 Find the mean of each pair of numbers.

   a 6, 20
   b 12, 30
   c 60, 90
   d 100, 500
   e 72, 24
   f 230, 180

2 Find the mean of these numbers.

Example
4, 8, 10, 14   Total = 4 + 8 + 10 + 14 = 36   36 ÷ 4 = 9 Mean = 9

   a 6, 9, 12
   b 4, 5, 9
   c 1, 1, 10
   d 7, 7, 7
   e 100, 20, 30
   f 0, 8, 10

3 Find the mean of these numbers.

   a 5, 5, 7, 7
   b 2, 0, 7, 7
   c 10, 10, 10, 50
   d 50, 100, 100, 150
   e 6, 12, 6, 12
   f 4, 19, 7, 2

4 Find the mean of these numbers.

   a 1, 4, 1, 4, 5
   b 5, 20, 30, 40, 5
   c 0, 0, 10, 20, 30
   d 10, 40, 50, 50, 100
   e 9, 0, 1, 0, 5
   f 500, 100, 200, 100, 100

Challenge

Find the median, mean and range of these values.

Hint: there may be two middle values.

You need:
• a calculator

1 25, 91, 63, 84, 32

2 324 g, 596 g, 280 g, 300 g, 146 g, 63 g, 92 g, 451 g

3 £1·25, £4·62, £5·88, £9·27, £16·41, £8·47

4 31·2 cm, 51·1 cm, 18·5 cm

5 400, 9000, 3500, 250, 850, 1250, 500, 7000, 6250, 4950

6 126 kg, 621 kg, 126 kg, 162 kg, 261 kg, 216 kg, 609 kg

7 319 ml, 913 ml, 139 ml, 319 ml

8 16 seconds, 94 seconds, 31 seconds, 75 seconds, 13 seconds

9 94p, £1·84, £1, 34p, 72p, £1·96, 50p, £1, £2·14, £5·16

10 3 m, 214 cm, 1·6 m, 91 cm, 2 m, 250 cm

More means

Practice

The database shows some information about hi-fi shops.

Shop	Cost of Crystal Hi-fi: (£)	Cost of JCV Hi-fi: (£)	Number of hi-fis in stock
Derrys	240	384	6
Asteroid	210	510	23
Connect	245	499	0
Tech Plus	220	377	5
Sounds	210	500	7
High Notes	260	499	5
Music World	225	500	3

Copy the database.

1 a Find the mode for each column.
  b Find the range for each column.
  c Find the mean for each column.
  d Find the median for each column.

2 a Which hi-fi has the highest mode of prices?
  b Which hi-fi has the lowest mean price?
  c Which hi-fi has the widest range of prices?
     What does this mean?

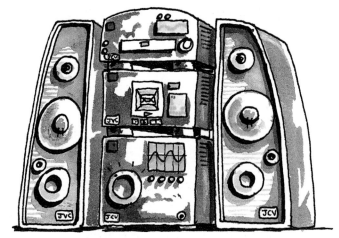

3 Add this entry to your database:

Tracks	210	499	5

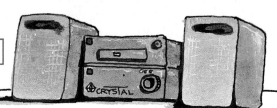

4 a Calculate the new median for each column.
  b Calculate the new mode and range for each column.
  c How has the median of prices of Crystal changed?
  d How has the mode of prices of JCV changed?
  e How do you think the mean prices have changed?
  f Calculate the new mean prices. Were you correct?

Refresher

1 Find the mode of these values (there may be two modes).
   a 4, 2, 6, 1, 2, 3, 8   b £42, £38, £40, £38, £42, £60
   c 300g, 350g, 200g, 150g, 200g, 250g, 50g, 350g

> **Hint**
> Mode = the most common value

2 Find the median of these values.
   a 9, 4, 4, 6, 1, 8, 3   b £210, £160, £400, £235, £92
   c 52g, 16g, 20g, 83g, 25g, 16g, 49g, 85g, 96g

> **Hint**
> Median = the middle value

3 Find the mean of these values.
   a 6, 9, 6   b 8, 5, 2, 9
   c £30, £70, £25, £50, £100
   d 23g, 41g, 32g, 75g, 83g, 25g, 46g, 19g

> **Hint**
> To find the mean, find the total, then divide by the number of values.

4 Find the range of these values.
   a 20, 5, 5, 10, 60, 40, 45
   b £7, £11, £2, £2, £9, £11, £3, £6
   c 315g, 261g, 180g, 592g, 149g, 176g, 251g, 832g, 612g, 180g

> **Hint**
> To find the range, subtract the smallest value from the largest value.

Challenge

1 Copy and complete the database for these packets of biscuits.
2 Calculate the mode, median, mean and range for each column.

 Ginger Snaps — 10 biscuits, 85p, 200g

 Cream Sandwich — 20 biscuits, £1·12, 500g

 Butter wheels — 8 biscuits, £1, 90g

Coconut Swirls — 12 biscuits, 70p, 160g

  Strawberry Hearts — 15 biscuits, 96p, 300g

Fruit Bars — 12 biscuits, £1·42, 180g

Chocolate Fingers — 10 biscuits, £1·20, 90g

 Lemon Drops — 10 biscuits, 75p, 200g

 Cherry Spots — 20 biscuits, £2·35, 700g

Name of biscuit	Number of biscuits	Price	Weight
Ginger Snaps	10	85p	200g

3-D edges and faces

Practice

The table is horizontal.

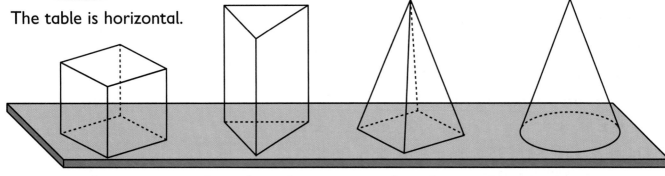

cube   triangular prism   square-based pyramid   cone

1 a For each shape, write the total number of faces.
   b Count the number of faces which are **horizontal** and which are **vertical**.

Copy and complete this table

> *Remember*
> In some shapes there will be faces which are neither horizontal or vertical.

Shape	Total number of faces	Horizontal faces	Vertical faces
cube	6	2	
triangular prism			
square pyramid			
cone			

2 Copy and complete this table for the edges of each shape.

Shape	Total number of edges	Horizontal edges	Vertical edges
cube	12		4
triangular prism			
square pyramid			
cone			

3 These shapes are on a horizontal surface.

   For each shape:

   a name 2 pairs of parallel edges.
   b name 4 pairs of perpendicular edges.
   c write the number of perpendicular faces.

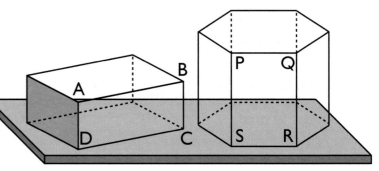

Refresher

This is a wall cupboard in the kitchen.

The corners of the door are labelled A, B, C and D.

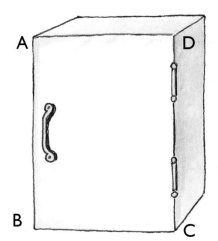

1 Copy and complete these sentences.

  a The horizontal edges are AD and ____.

  b The vertical edges are ____ and ____.

  c Edge AD is parallel to ____.

  d Edge ____ is parallel to AB.

2 Name 2 pairs of perpendicular edges.

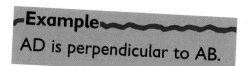

Example

AD is perpendicular to AB.

Challenge

These shapes are on a horizontal table.

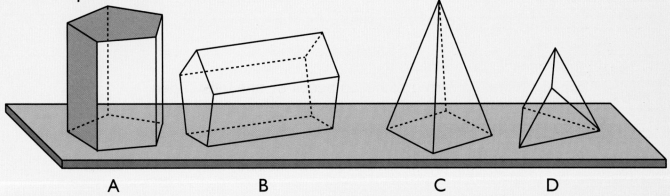

Work with a partner.

1 a Make a table to list the number of **horizontal** and **perpendicular** faces for each pentagonal prism (shapes A and B) and each square-based pyramid (shapes C and D).

  b Compare your answers for the pentagonal prisms, then for the square-based pyramids.

  Write what you notice.

2 a Make a table to list the number of pairs of parallel edges for each shape.

  b Write what you notice about your answers to shapes A and B, then shapes C and D.

Parallelogram and rhombus

Practice

You need:
- 1 cm dot square paper
- coloured pencil or pen

A parallelogram has its opposite sides equal and parallel.

A rhombus is a parallelogram with 4 equal sides.

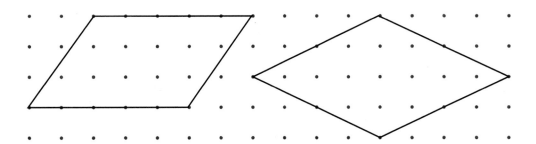

1 On 1 cm dot square paper draw:

a 5 different parallelograms

b 5 different rhombi

2 Write the name, **parallelogram** or **rhombus** beneath each shape.

3 Check each shape for line symmetry.

Rule the axis of symmetry with a coloured pencil or fine felt-tip pen.

4 Copy and complete this table.

Write ✓ for *yes* and ✗ for *no*.

Quadrilateral	Opposite sides equal	Opposite sides parallel	Opposite angles equal	All sides equal	All right angles
rectangle					
square					
parallelogram					
rhombus					

Refresher

Write in which region you would put these shapes.

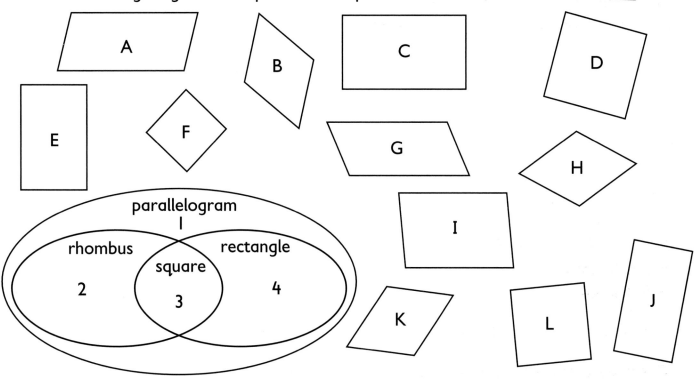

Challenge

For each pair of quadrilaterals, write 1 way in which they are similar and 1 way in which they are different.

Copy and complete this table.

Quadrilaterals	Similar properties	Different properties
square and rectangle	both have 4 right angles	square has 4 equal sides rectangle has opposite sides equal
square and rhombus		
rectangle and parallelogram		
rhombus and parallelogram		

Trapezium and kite

Practice

1 Name each shape.

2 Write the letter of each shape which has:

    a only one pair of opposite parallel sides

    b 2 pairs of adjacent sides equal

    c only one line of symmetry

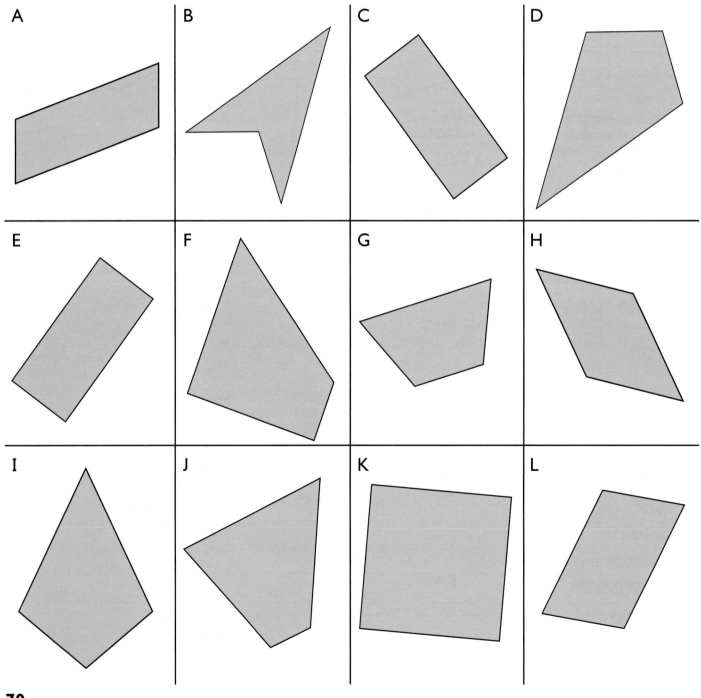

A   B   C   D

E   F   G   H

I   J   K   L

Refresher

A trapezium has one pair of opposite parallel sides.

A kite has 2 pairs of adjacent sides equal

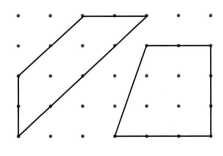
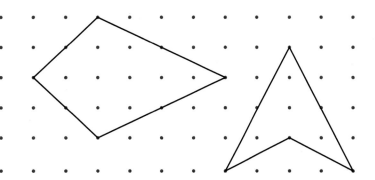

1 On 1 cm dot square paper draw:

a 5 different trapezia

b 5 different kites

2 Write the name **trapezium** or **kite** beneath each shape.

Challenge

Jigsaw trapezia

1 Draw 4 congruent trapezia on triangular dot square paper.

Cut out the shapes.

Assemble the 4 trapezia to make one large trapezium.

2 Draw and cut out 8 more trapezia.

Assemble all 8 trapezia to make one large trapezium.

3 Compare the large trapezia you made in questions 1 and 2.

What can you say about their areas?

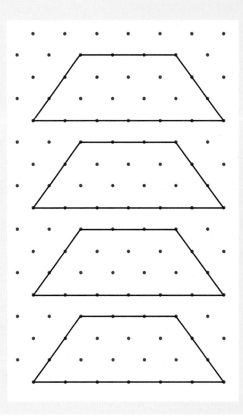

Investigating diagonals

Practice

1 Copy these quadrilaterals on to 1 cm squared paper.

2 Draw in the diagonals and cut out each shape.

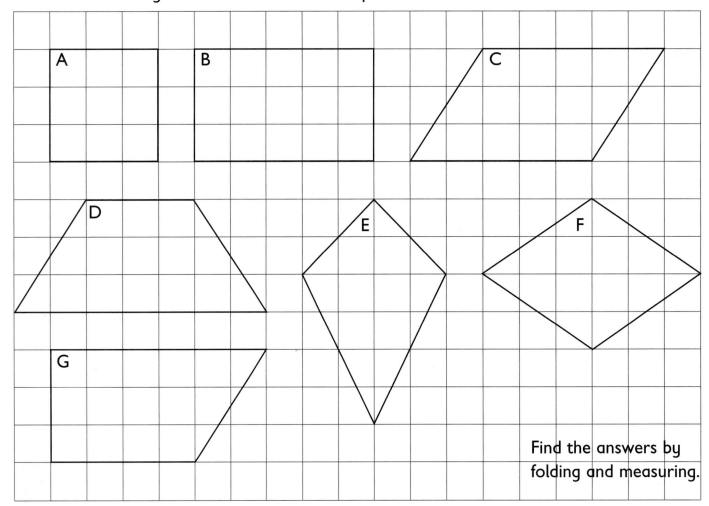

Find the answers by folding and measuring.

3 Copy and complete. Mark ✓ for *yes* and ✗ for *no*.

Property	Quadrilateral						
	A	B	C	D	E	F	G
4 sides equal	✓	✗	✗				
4 angles equal	✓						
diagonals are same length							
diagonals cut each other in half							
diagonals intersect at right angles							
a diagonal is an axis of symmetry							

Refresher

1 Copy each quadrilateral on to 1cm squared paper.

2 Draw in the diagonals.

3 Below each shape write its name.

4 Colour red the diagonals which intersect at right angles.

quadrilateral names:
square, rectangle, rhombus, trapezium, parallelogram, kite

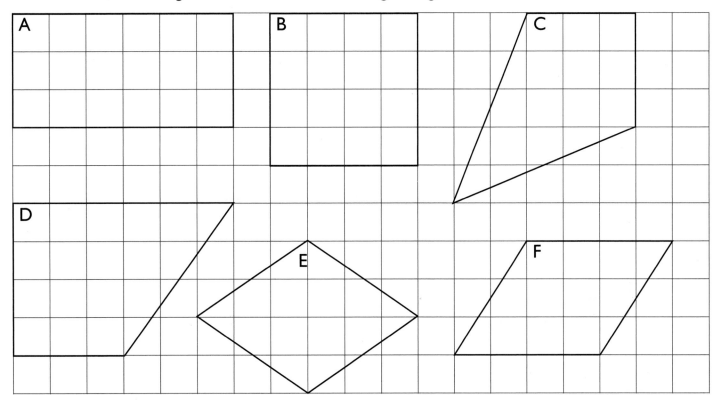

Challenge

Diagonals of rectangles and parallelograms.

1 Investigate this statement.

The diagonals of any rectangle are equal and bisect each other.

2 Draw about 6 different parallelograms on dot square paper. Draw in the diagonals. For each parallelogram, measure the diagonals from the vertex to the intersection. Write what you notice.

3 Compare your results for questions 1 and 2.

In what ways are the diagonals of rectangles and parallelograms similar? Different?

Co-ordinating shapes

You need:
● a copy of Resource Copymaster 17

Practice

1 List the vertices and co-ordinates of

   a   square ABCD

   b   rectangle EFGH

   c   parallelogram KLMN

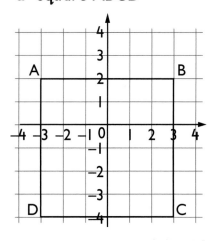
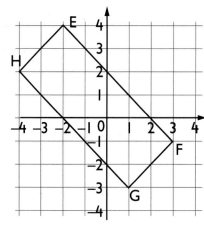
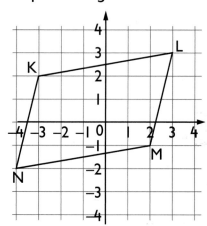

2 Plot these points on Resource Copymaster 17.

   A (2, 3), B (−3, 4), C (2, −4), D (−5, −5), E (0, −4), F (−6, 0), and G (2, 3)

   Name the points which are:

   a   in the 2nd quadrant   b   in the third quadrant   c   in the 4th quadrant

   d   on the x-axis   e   on the y-axis

3 On Resource Copymaster 17 plot these points and join them up in order.
   Name each shape you draw.

   a   (−2, 1), (−2, 3), (3, 1), (3, 3)   b   (−3, 2), (0, 4), (3, 2), (0, −3)

4 The points H (−3, 3), I (3, 2) and J (2, −4) are three of the four vertices of a square.

   Plot the points and join them up in order.

   Find the 4th vertex K and write its co-ordinates.

5 a   Plot these points and join them up in order.

      P (1, 1), Q (2, 3), R (1, 5) and S (6, 3).

   b   Plot the reflection of PQRS in the y-axis.
      Name the co-ordinates of the reflected shape.

Refresher

1 A game at the school fair is guessing where the treasure is buried.

Copy the grid on to squared paper.

Complete this list of guesses.

A (−5, __)

B (__, 4)

C (−4, __)

D (__, 3)

E (__, __)

F (__, __)

G (__, __)

H (__, __)

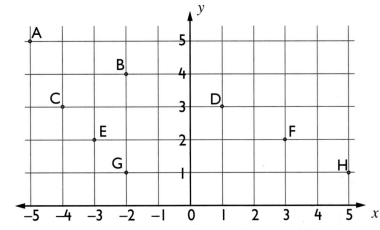

2 Four unclaimed prizes are buried at these points.

Plot the points on the co-ordinate grid.

P1 (−2, 3), P2 (2, 1), P3 (−3, 1), P4 (3, 5)

Challenge

Investigate the patterns in the co-ordinates of triangle ABC

a reflected into the 4 quadrants

b rotated into the 4 quadrants about the origin.

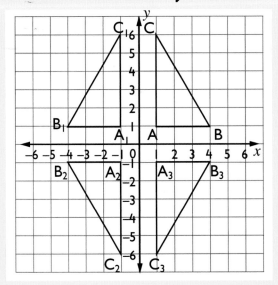

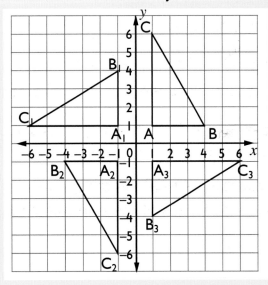

Translating patterns

Practice

Example

Grid 1

a This table shows the co-ordinates for the corresponding vertices of the shape.

	x-axis	y-axis
shape A	−2	6
shape B	1	5
shape C	4	4

b The shape is translated 3 to the right, then 1 down.

c The next two rows in the table are:

shape D   7   3
shape E   10   2

1 For each of the grids 2 to 4:
  a copy and complete a table for the corresponding vertices.
  b write the distance and the direction of the translation, e.g. 3 to the right then 1 down.
  c write the next two rows for each table.

2 Explain the connection between the translated shapes and the pattern of corresponding vertices.

3 a Design a different translating pattern for the shape and draw 3 translations on Resource Copymaster 16.
  b Choose a corresponding vertex for each shape and write their co-ordinates in a table.
  c Describe the translation.
  d Complete the next two rows in the table.

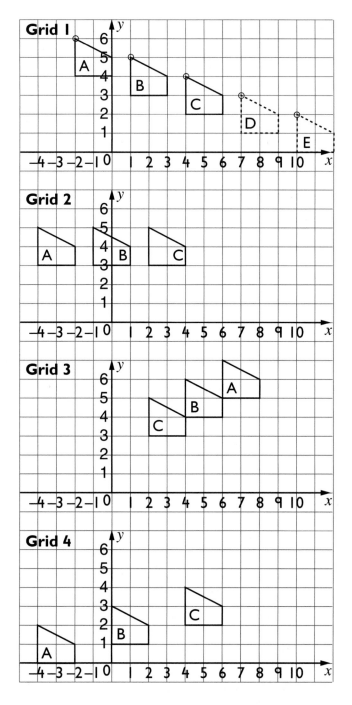

76

Refresher

Grid 1

The first shape is drawn in each grid.

Copy these shapes on to Resource Copymaster 15.

Plot the points of a second shape in each grid.

Join the points in order.

Then complete the sentence for each translation.

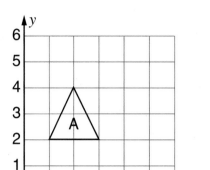

a Plot these points in grid 1 to make shape B.

(4, 3) (5, 5) (6, 3)

Shape A has been translated __ to the right,
then __ up.

Grid 2

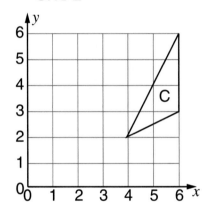

b Plot these points in grid 2 to make shape D.

(0, 1) (2, 5) (2, 2)

Shape D has been translated ___ to the left,
then __ down.

Challenge

1 Translate the quadrilateral using the rule: 2 to the right, then 2 up.
Then translate the quadrilateral using the rule: 3 to the right, then 1 down.

2 Continue the translations, alternating between each one until you have filled the grid.

3 Use one colour only for each translation.

4 Write about the pattern you notice.

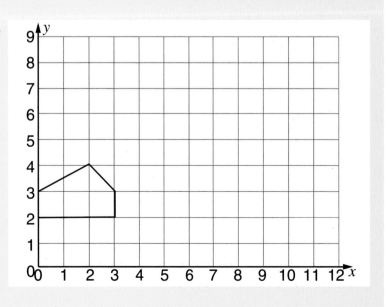

Sliding shapes

Practice

1 Name the shape in each overlap of two congruent right-angled isosceles triangles.

a   b   c

d   e   f

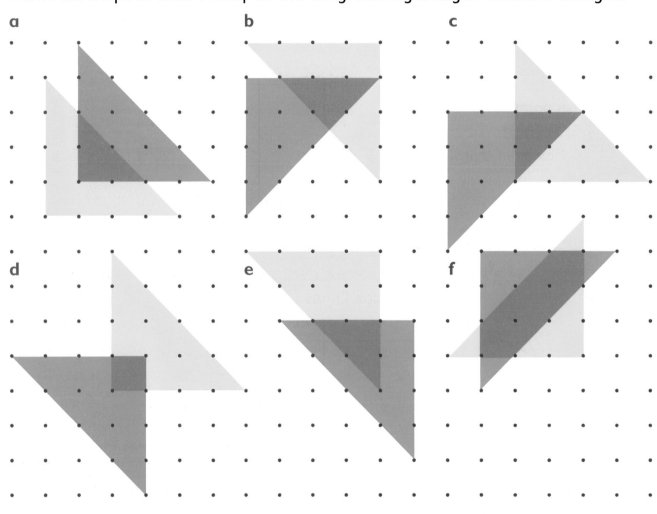

2 Write in which of the above arrangements a triangle was:

   a   translated   b   rotated

3 Find different overlapping shapes using the same size of triangles as in question 1.
Record on 1 cm square dot grid paper.
Remember you can translate, rotate or reflect the triangles.
Here are some ideas:

   a   rectangle   b   large square

   c   large parallelogram   d   trapezium

   e   2 different pentagons

Refresher

1 Name the shape in each overlap of 2 congruent equilateral triangles.

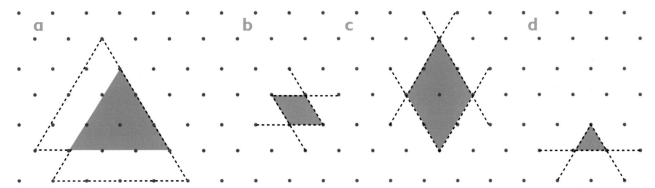

a   b   c

2 These diagrams show the overlap made by 2 congruent equilateral triangles.

For each diagram:

a Draw the overlap on 1 cm dot triangular paper.

b Work out how the 2 equilateral triangles were placed to create the overlap and complete each drawing.

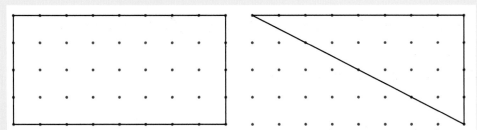

a   b   c   d

Challenge

You have a rectangle and a right-angled triangle.

Investigate the different overlapping shapes you can make with these shapes.
Record your overlapping shapes on 1 cm dot square paper.

Calculating perimeters

Practice

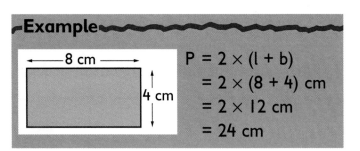
1 Use the formula to work out the perimeter of these rectangles.

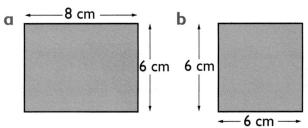

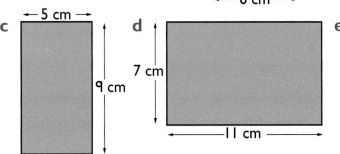

2 Work out the perimeter of these shapes.

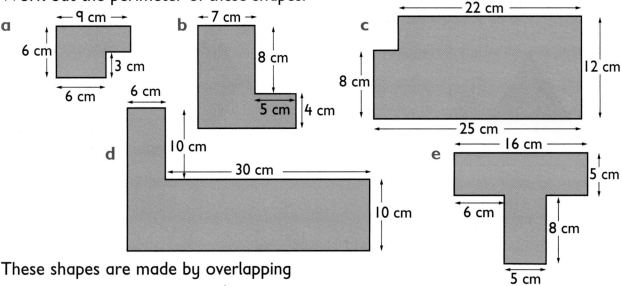

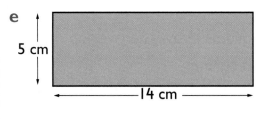

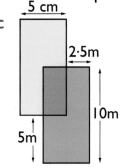

3 These shapes are made by overlapping congruent squares or rectangles.
   Find a way to work out the perimeter of each shaded shape.

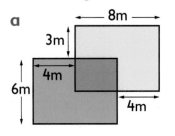

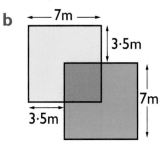

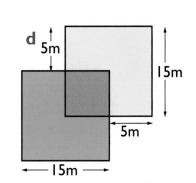

Refresher

Each shape is an edge to edge arrangement of 6 squares.
Find a way to work out the perimeter of each shape.

Example

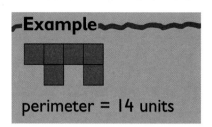

perimeter = 14 units

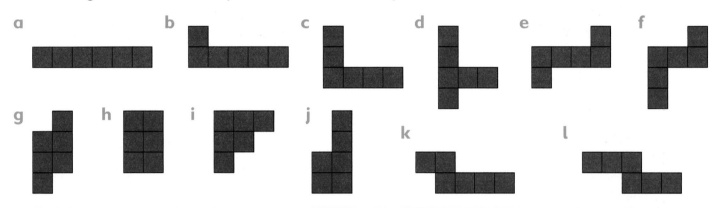

a   b   c   d   e   f

g   h   i   j   k   l

Challenge

1 Copy these staircases on to 1 cm squared paper.

2 Find the perimeter of each staircase in centimetres.

3 Draw the next two staircases in the sequence.

For 1 step
P = 4 cm

For 2 steps
P = _____ cm

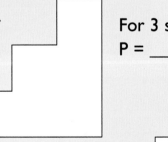

For 3 steps
P = _____ cm

For 4 steps
P = _____ cm

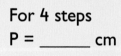

4 Enter your results in a table.

number of steps in staircase	1	2	3	4	5	6
perimeter of staircase	4					

5 Using the pattern, predict the perimeter of a 10 step staircase.... a 100 step staircase.

Connecting midpoints

Practice

1 In triangle ABC
the midpoint of
each side is marked.
   a Measure the line AB to the
   nearest millimetre.
   b Now measure the midpoint line
   parallel to AB.
   c Compare your answers.
   Write what you notice about
   the two lengths.

2 Repeat the steps in question 1 for
lines AC and BC.

3 a Copy this rectangle on to 1 cm
   squared paper.
   b Measure and calculate the
   perimeter of the inner and
   outer rectangles.
   c Write what you notice about
   the 2 lengths.
   d Draw a different rectangle.
   Join the pairs of midpoints until
   you make the inner rectangle.
   Measure and compare their
   perimeters.

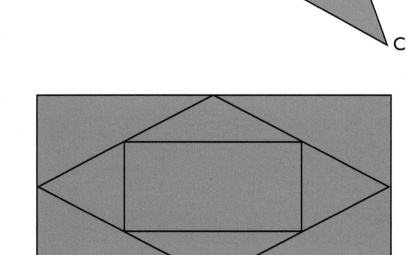

4 a Draw this rhombus on 1 cm
   squared paper.
   b Compare the lengths of pairs of
   parallel sides as in question 1.
   c Record your findings.
   d Draw another rhombus and
   repeat as before.

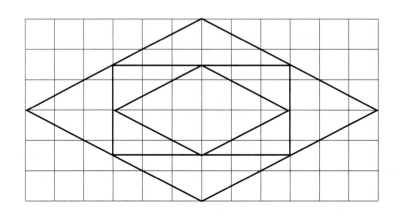

Refresher

1 In each triangle, measure to the nearest millimetre, the two parallel sides.

Write your answers in centimetres, for example, write 47 mm as 4·7 cm

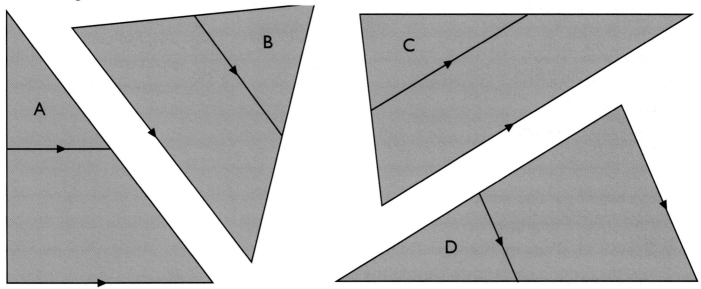

2 On 1 cm squared paper, draw 3 different right-angled triangles.

Join the midpoints of 2 sides. Measure the 2 parallel sides, recording as above.

Challenge

1 On 1 cm squared paper, draw 3 different
   parallelograms.
   For each parallelogram:
   ● join the sets of midpoints as in the
     diagram.
   ● compare the perimeters of the smallest
     and largest parallelograms.

2 Write about the relationship you notice.

3 Now draw 3 different isosceles trapezia.
   Compare the lengths of pairs of parallel
   sides.
   Write what you notice.

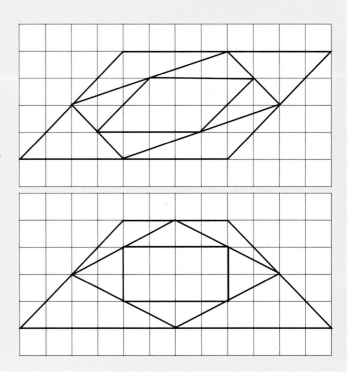

Pinboards, parallels and perimeters

Practice

Criteria checklist:

a Name the shape.

b Mark the parallel sides. >>

c Mark the right angles. ⌐

d Use the same colour for each pair of parallel lines.

e Count the pins on the perimeter.

f Draw any lines of symmetry.

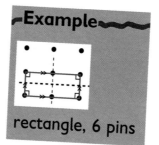

Example

rectangle, 6 pins

You need:

● a copy of Resource Copymaster 12
● a ruler
● coloured pencils or felt-tip pens

1 Two pairs of parallel sides.

a Find 6 more shapes which have 2 pairs of parallel sides.

b Draw each shape on Resource Copymaster 12.

c Use the criteria checklist to classify the shape.

d Write the name and the number of perimeter pins below each shape.

2 Three pairs of parallel sides.

Find and draw 3 shapes which have 3 pairs of parallel sides.

Repeat the steps b to d of question 2.

3 How many different polygons can you make in your pinboard which have no parallel sides?

Investigate.

Refresher

a Draw this quadrilateral on your pinboard sheet.
b Mark the parallel sides. >>
c Mark the right angles. ⌐
d Colour the equal sides red.
e Name the shape.

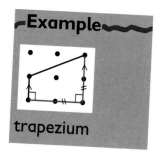

Example

trapezium

You need:
● a copy of Resource Copymaster 12
● a ruler
● coloured pencils or felt-tip pens

1 Repeat the steps above for these quadrilaterals.

a   b   c

2 Find and draw 3 pentagons which have one pair of parallel sides.

Challenge

You need half a sheet of 1 cm dot square paper.
Rule lines to make twelve 4 × 4 pinboards.

1 Make 6 different polygons with 2 pairs of parallel sides.

2 Make 3 different polygons with 3 pairs of parallel sides.

3 Make 3 octagons where every side is parallel to at least one more side.

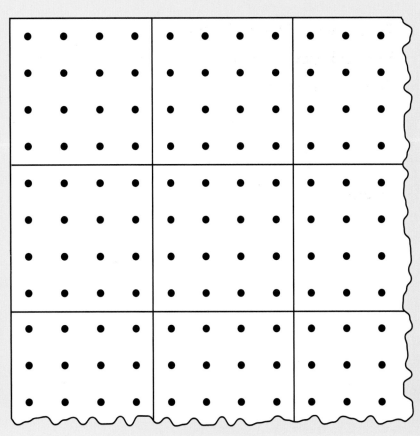

World times

Practice

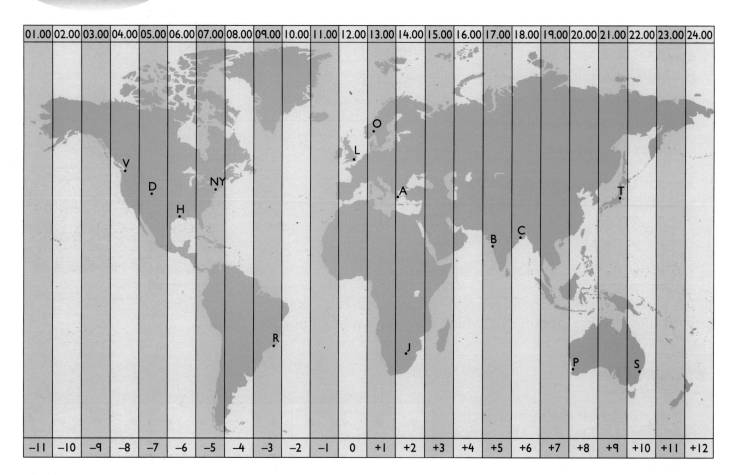

| 01.00 | 02.00 | 03.00 | 04.00 | 05.00 | 06.00 | 07.00 | 08.00 | 09.00 | 10.00 | 11.00 | 12.00 | 13.00 | 14.00 | 15.00 | 16.00 | 17.00 | 18.00 | 19.00 | 20.00 | 21.00 | 22.00 | 23.00 | 24.00 |

| −11 | −10 | −9 | −8 | −7 | −6 | −5 | −4 | −3 | −2 | −1 | 0 | +1 | +2 | +3 | +4 | +5 | +6 | +7 | +8 | +9 | +10 | +11 | +12 |

1 It is 12 noon in London. In which city is the time:

   a 6 a.m.   b 21:00   c 04:00   d 10 p.m.

2 Write the time differences in hours between these cities:

   a New York and Athens   b Rio de Janeiro and Perth
   c Vancouver and Oslo   d Denver and Johannesburg

3 It is 8:30 p.m. in Athens. Write the time it is in:

   a London   b Houston
   c Calcutta   d Tokyo

4 It is 04:15 Saturday in Sydney. What is the time and day in:

   a Calcutta   b London   c New York   d Perth

5 Your flight for Vancouver leaves Tokyo at 12:00 on a Thursday.
   What day is it in Vancouver?

Refresher

Use your world time chart to help you.

1 It is 12:00 in London.

Write the time it is in these cities in two ways:

a Athens   b Denver   c Calcutta   d Perth

e Houston   f Rio de Janeiro   g Tokyo   h Oslo

2 Name a city which is:

a 2 hours ahead of London b 5 hours behind London

c 9 hours ahead of London d 8 hours behind London

e 7 hours behind London   f 10 hours ahead of London

Challenge

Key

B   Banff
C   Chicago
D   Denver
H   Houston
M   Miami
NY New York
S   Seattle
SF San Francisco
T   Toronto

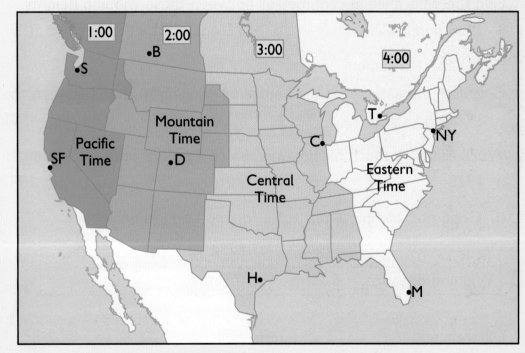

Choose a city in each time zone to set up offices for your computer company.

1 Your London head office works from 09:00 to 17:00.
   Write the times during which each of your American offices can phone London.

2 In America work begins at 7:30 a.m.
   It is cheaper to phone America after 12:00.
   For each American office, draw up a list of phone times which can use
   the cheaper rate.

Winning distances

Practice

These are the winning distances for men and women at four Olympic Games.

Look at the results for High Jump – Men

Year	1896	1928
Winning height	1·81 m	1·94 m

Difference 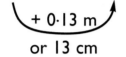 + 0·13 m

or 13 cm

		Men	Women
High Jump	1896	1·81m	•
	1928	1·94m	1·59m
	1972	2·29m	1·93m
	1992	2·34m	2·02m
Long Jump	1896	6·35m	•
	1928	7·73m	•
	1972	8·24m	6·78m
	1992	8·67m	7·75m

1   High Jump – Men

Find the difference in centimetres between these winning heights:

a 1928 and 1972   b 1972 and 1992   c 1928 and 1992

2   High Jump – Women

Calculate in centimetres the improved winning heights between these years:

a 1928 and 1972   b 1972 and 1992   c 1928 and 1992

3   Work out how much higher the men could jump than the women in:

a 1928   b 1972   c 1992

4   a   Copy and complete this table for the Long Jump – Men

Year	1896	1928	1972	1992
Winning distance	6·35 m	7·73 m	_____	_____

Difference   1·38 m   _____   _____

b How much longer was the winning jump in 1992 than 1896?

5   Compare the winning jumps for men and women in the Olympic Games of

a 1972   b 1992

Refresher

a Measure each see-saw to the nearest millimetre.
b Calculate the distance from an end to the midpoint of the see-saw. Write your answer: in millimetres, then in centimetres.

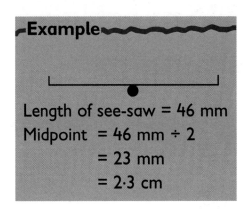

Length of see-saw = 46 mm
Midpoint = 46 mm ÷ 2
= 23 mm
= 2·3 cm

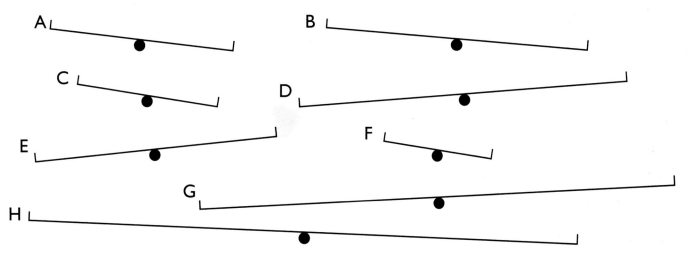

Challenge

Gerry has a jumping bean.

He rules a number line and places the bean at point A.

1 The bean jumps on to B,
2 then halfway back to A, landing on 6.
3 The bean jumps halfway towards B, landing on 7,
4 then halfway back to A, landing on 5·5.

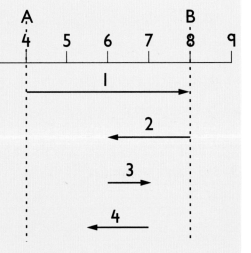

1 Where will the bean land after a halfway jump towards B and then a halfway jump back to A?

2 Draw a number line from 1 to 10.
Find a different starting number for your jumping bean.
Work out where your bean will land after a total of 6 halfway forward and backward jumps.

3 What if the first jump was from 3 to 8?

89

Converting units of length

Practice

Bill found these lengths of wood in his garden hut.

1 Find the length of each strip of wood in metres.

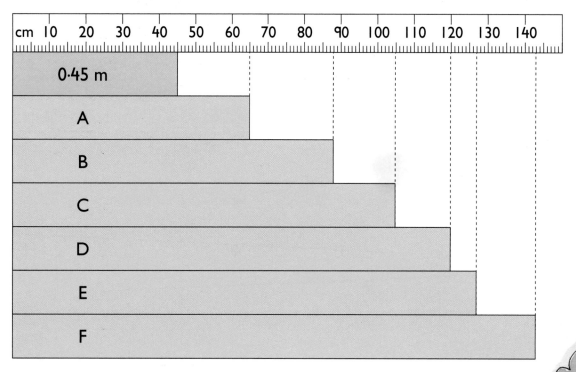

2 Find the difference in length in cm:
   a between A and D
   b between B and E
   c between C and F

3 Find the total length in metres of these strips of wood.
   a A and E   b B and F
   c C and B   d D and F

4 Bill cuts strip D into 8 equal lengths.
   How many millimetres long is each piece of wood?

5 Bill's farm is 1·5 km from the main road. The council is resurfacing his farm road.
   Before lunch the workmen had resurfaced half of the distance.
   After lunch they had covered half of the remaining distance when the rain began to fall.
   Tomorrow, if it is dry, they will finish the job.
   How many metres of road surfaces will they have to complete tomorrow?

Refresher

1 Write how far each child cycled in kilometres.

Tony   3725 m   Tom   4420 m

Kim   5010 m   Kate   3205 m

2 Write how far each child swam in metres.

Kenny   0·725 km   Chris   0·408 km

Terry   0·57 km   Ted   0·6 km

3 Write these lengths in centimetres.

   a 16 mm   b 42 mm   c 1·6 m   d 4·2 m

Challenge

A patio is 3 m long and 1 m wide.

You have a supply of paving stones which are 1 m long and 0·5 m wide.

How many different arrangements of paving stones can you make?

Begin like this:

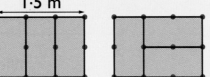

For a path 0·5 m long   1 way

For a path 1·0 m long   2 ways

For a path 1·5 m long   3 ways

The answer for a path 2·0 m long is NOT 4!

1 a Draw the paths on squared or dot paper until you see a pattern.

   b Write in words how the pattern works.

2 What if the patio was 5 metres long.

   How many different arrangements of paving stones could you make?

Converting miles to kilometres

Practice

1 Copy and complete this table.

Miles	0	5	10	15	20	25
Kilometres	0	8				
Co-ordinates	(0, 0)	(5, 8)				

2 Plot the points on to graph paper.

Join the points with a ruler and sharp pencil.

Extend the straight line as far as it will go.

3 Find the equivalent distances from your graph.

    a 30 miles   **b** 40 miles   **c** 45 miles

    d 64 km   **e** 56 km   **f** 72 km

4 At point **a** on the straight line, 12 km converts to 7·5 miles.

Copy and complete for these points on the line.

    b 16 km ≈ _____ miles

    c ___ km ≈ _____ miles

    d ___ km ≈ _____ miles

    e ___ km ≈ _____ miles

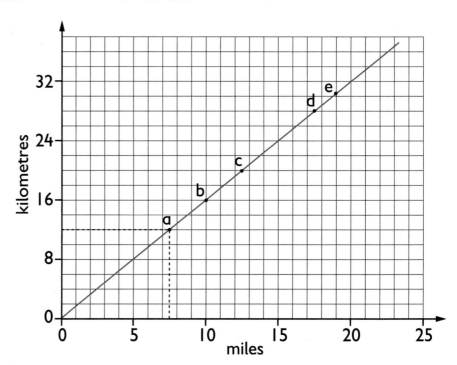

5 If 5 miles convert to 8 kilometres, then 50 miles convert to 80 kilometres.

Convert these distances to kilometres.

    a 100 miles   **b** 250 miles   **c** 450 miles   **d** 505 miles

Convert these distances to miles.

    e 240 km   **f** 640 km   **g** 480 km   **g** 1000 km

Refresher

1 Copy and complete this table.

Miles	0	5	10	15
Kilometres	0	8		
Co-ordinates	(0, 0)	(5, 8)		

2 a Use graph paper to plot the points from your table.

b Using a ruler and sharp pencil, join the points.

c Continue the straight line until it runs off your graph.

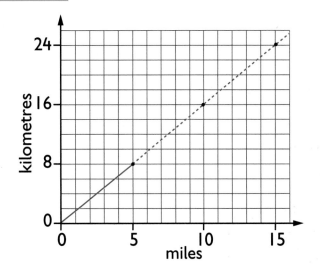

3 Use your graph to answer these questions.

a 4 km ≈ ___ miles

b 12 km ≈ ____ miles

c 20 km ≈ ___ miles

d 4 miles ≈ ____ km

Challenge

During their Canadian holiday, two couples hired a camper van for one week.
Bill drove 50% of the total distance.
His wife Frances drove half as far as the combined distance driven by the other couple.
Jack drove 4 times as far as his wife Betty.
Betty drove for 80 kilometres.

a How many kilometres did each person drive?

b What was the total distance, in miles, of their Canadian holiday?

Festive length

Practice

1 The Lindsay family is going to the Pantomime in town.
   They travel 3·6 km by car to the 'Park and Ride', 43·42 km by coach to town and walk 700 m to the theatre.
   a How many kilometres do they travel on the journey to the theatre?
   b How many kilometres is the round trip, to and from the theatre?

2 The pantomime beanstalk is 10 m high. Leaves are stuck to the stalk in 60 cm intervals.
   Jack has climbed to the 7th leaf from the ground.
   a What is his height from the ground?
   b How far has he still to climb to reach the top of the beanstalk?

3 Jack's footprint is 245 mm. The giant's footprint is 8 times as long.
   Find the length of the giant's footprint: a in centimetres
   b in metres

4 The giant makes his own shoelaces. Each lace is 75 cm long.
   a How many pairs of laces can he make from a narrow strip of leather 10 m long?
   b How much leather will be left over?

5 Jack needs some rope to tether the golden goose.
   He says, "If I take a length of rope from box A and join it to one from box B, I can make 9 different lengths."
   True or false?

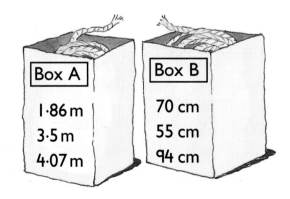

Box A	Box B
1·86 m	70 cm
3·5 m	55 cm
4·07 m	94 cm

Refresher

This photograph of the McDougall children is for Gran.

Alex wrote their heights at the bottom so that Gran could see how much they had grown.

Example
Alex is _____ m taller than Bob.

Alex	Bob	Chris	Derek	Ellen
1·44 m	1·25 m	1·39 m	1·51 m	96 cm

1 Find in **metres** the difference in height between:

   a Alex and Bob   b Alex and Chris   c Alex and Derek   d Alex and Ellen

2 Find in **centimetres** the difference between the tallest and shortest children.

3 Who is 14 cm taller than Bob?

Challenge

Chimney pot challenge

It is Christmas Eve. Santa has to visit every house in this street.

To save time he must start at one end of the street and finish at the other.

The street plan shows the distance between chimney pots.

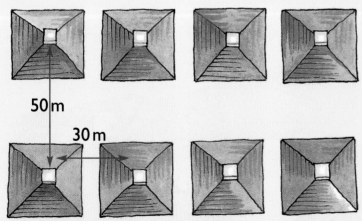

50 m

30 m

1 a Work out the shortest route for Santa.

   b Find the total length of the shortest route down this street.

2 What if there were 6 houses on either side of the street?

In your head

Practice

Work out all these calculations in your head.

You can use the strategy suggested or use your own.

1 Work these out in your head by counting up.

    a 8000 − 2994   b 7006 − 3993   c 9008 − 5991   d 6012 − 1989   e 5015 − 2987

    f 9000 − 4978   g 8005 − 992   h 6014 − 1978   i 7001 − 6975   j 10 000 − 8997

2 Use rounding to the nearest multiple of 100 or 1000 to work out these calculations.

    a 486 + 94   b 797 − 196   c 301 + 594   d 516 + 602   e 1429 − 499

    f 2672 − 503   g 5810 + 607   h 9012 − 1395   i 6375 + 1599   j 7587 − 1998

3 Round the second decimal to the nearest whole number, then adjust.

    a 6·8 + 1·9   b 5·3 − 2·1   c 2·3 + 3·1   d 5·6 + 2·9   e 10·3 − 4·1

    f 6·7 + 3·9   g 8·3 + 5·1   h 9·8 − 4·9   i 3·6 + 8·1   j 7·5 − 1·1

4 Partition the numbers into hundreds, tens and units to help you add them.

    a 586 + 297   b 784 + 406   c 219 + 513   d 651 + 286   e 784 + 173

    f 612 + 850   g 973 + 462   h 481 + 554   i 375 + 902   j 657 + 812

Refresher

1 Partition the numbers into hundreds, tens and units to help you add them.

a 286 + 163   b 315 + 206   c 172 + 197   d 368 + 508   e 291 + 265

f 406 + 372   g 472 + 337   h 554 + 256   i 583 + 242   j 675 + 185

2 Count up from the second number to work out these subtractions.

a 203 – 95   b 506 – 296   c 701 – 394

d 600 – 295   e 504 – 196   f 307 – 99

g 801 – 591   h 906 – 498   i 800 – 296

j 507 – 199

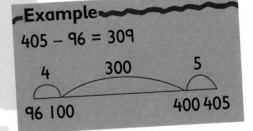

Example
405 – 96 = 309

3 Round the second number to the nearest multiple of 10 or 100 to help work out these calculations.

a 286 + 98   b 412 – 89   c 352 + 95

d 563 – 194   e 484 + 199   f 561 – 201

g 376 + 104   h 567 – 205   i 491 + 304

j 673 – 202

Example
147 + 79 = 226
147 + 80 = 227
227 – 1 = 226

Challenge

Choose two calculations from each section of the Practice page.
Explain in writing how you worked them out in your head.

Vertical addition

Practice

Write out these calculations vertically and then work out the answer.

1 a 19623 + 765   b 58721 + 491   c 67529 + 780   d 56721 + 563   e 48935 + 609
   f 34627 + 721   g 80941 + 586   h 61824 + 638   i 57638 + 279   j 73706 + 973

2 a 16724 + 5138   b 26849 + 2816   c 59371 + 3499   d 29726 + 6081   e 35862 + 7729
   f 73892 + 5637   g 63715 + 5273   h 91863 + 6415   i 55985 + 9073   j 48212 + 1976

3 a 407·7 + 58·63   b 512·2 + 97·65   c 267·1 + 98·24   d 365·9 + 78·94   e 683·4 + 95·72
   f 987·2 + 58·14   g 487·5 + 75·73   h 871·9 + 48·72   i 451·4 + 75·91   j 861·7 + 29·67

Refresher

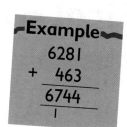

Example

```
  6281
+  463
  6744
    1
```

1 Copy out these calculations and then work out the answer.

a	5962 + 307	b	7831 + 189	c	6214 + 863	d	8931 + 749	e	4727 + 535

f	3861 + 486	g	2972 + 408	h	6175 + 362	i	5096 + 872	j	7243 + 574

2 Write these calculations vertically and then work them out.

a	1672 + 2384	b	3641 + 5283	c	2765 + 2064	d	5267 + 5351	e	4821 + 3758

f	5137 + 4575	g	4819 + 2345	h	7672 + 1609	i	8019 + 3425	j	3862 + 4638

Challenge

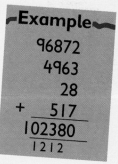

Example

```
  96872
   4963
     28
+   517
 102380
   1212
```

Add these numbers using the vertical method.

```
a    56842        b      189        c    95412
      658                67               86
     1473             84791             3647
+      63         +    4862        +     284
```

```
d       47        e    60247
      5847             2380
     36568              743
+      842        +      95
```

Vertical subtraction

Practice

Write these calculations out vertically and then work out the answer.

1 a 94862 − 2394   b 38721 − 3282   c 97621 − 4265   d 73862 − 5135
   e 59124 − 5305   f 48728 − 6809   g 72616 − 7234   h 63704 − 7617
   i 49932 − 6341   j 51667 − 2571

2 a 72643 − 6249   b 58162 − 3714   c 64851 − 5206   d 96720 − 3167
   e 53384 − 7192   f 86124 − 9517   g 73561 − 2874   h 25962 − 8175
   i 32149 − 6072   j 49652 − 8572

3 a 109·7 − 27·36   b 206·3 − 36·21   c 591·7 − 61·83   d 671·4 − 55·73
   e 214·6 − 96·28   f 585·5 − 73·24   g 721·2 − 90·38   h 961·8 − 47·29
   i 638·9 − 47·65   j 372·1 − 83·91   k 465·6 − 95·31   l 392·6 − 41·32

Example
```
    6 1
  48̶7̶2
−  515
  ────
  4357
```

Refresher

1 Copy out these calculations and then work out the answer.

	a	b	c	d	e
	9638	4721	8672	5148	7637
	− 481	− 652	− 281	− 563	− 271

	f	g	h	i	j
	6249	9178	4482	7963	8721
	− 503	− 639	− 721	− 380	− 473

2 Write these calculations vertically and then work them out.

a 5863 − 2171   b 6973 − 3185   c 8962 − 4071   d 5163 − 2945   e 7948 − 2663

f 9617 − 3842   g 7293 − 1637   h 5541 − 3094   i 8761 − 3261   j 6174 − 2536

Challenge

How many subtraction calcuations can you make using these numbers?

a 14867   b 9872   c 27863   d 4893   e 35621   f 7814

Travel problems

Practice

1 One bus holds 52 people.

   a How many people can 6 buses hold? 8 buses?
      12 buses? 20 buses?

   b How many buses does a school need to hire to take
      out 126 children? 251 children? 308 children? 467 children?

2 Work out the price of the following tickets:

   a 4 tickets to York.

   b 3 tickets to Penzance

   c 5 tickets to Manchester.

   d 1 ticket to York and 1 ticket to Manchester

   e 1 ticket to Penzance and 1 ticket to Manchester.

> ### Rail prices
> London to York £56·48
> London to Penzance £64·18
> London to Manchester £37·96

3 Work out the length of these journeys.

   a Leeds to Edinburgh and back to Leeds.

   b Cardiff to London to Nottingham.

   c Leeds to Nottingham to London and back
      to Nottingham.

   d London to Nottingham and back.

> ### Distances:
> Nottingham to Leeds 97 km
> Leeds to Edinburgh 257 km
> London to Nottingham 153 km
> Cardiff to London 205 km

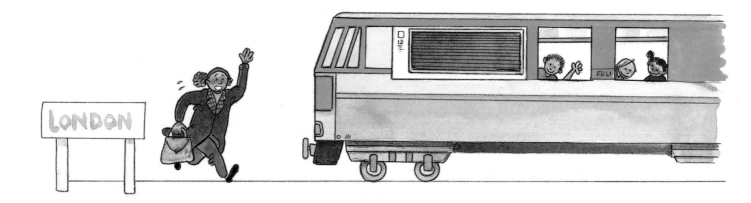

Refresher

Single bus fares from my house:

School 35p

Cinema 87p

Swimming pool £1·25

Shopping centre £1·48

1 Work out the price of the following journeys:
  a to the swimming pool and back
  b 3 tickets to the shopping centre
  c 6 tickets to the cinema
  d 10 tickets to school

2 Work out how many tickets I bought when I spent:
  a £2·45 on tickets to school
  b £4·35 on tickets to the cinema
  c £6·25 on tickets to the swimming pool
  d £2·96 on tickets to the shopping centre

3 Work out how much change I will get if I pay for:
  a a ticket to the cinema with a £5 note
  b a ticket to the swimming pool with a £5 note
  c a ticket to the shopping centre with a £10 note
  d a ticket to school with a £2 coin

Challenge

I have three piles of coins. Work out how many coins in each pile if:

  a The second pile has 3 more than the first, the third has three more than the second and there are 27 coins altogether.

  b The first pile has 9 more than the second, the third has 1 less than the second and there are 41 coins altogether.

  c The second pile has twice as many as the first, the third has twice as many as the second and there are 56 coins altogether.

School problems

Work out the problems. Record the calculations and say how you worked them out: in your head, in your head with jottings, with a calculator, using the vertical method.

Practice

Ingleton Primary School has 57 nursery children, 193 Keystage 1 children and 248 Keystage 2 children.

1 a How many children in Keystage 1 and Keystage 2?

   b All the 8 Keystage 2 classes have the same number of children. How many in each class?

   c The school has 22 places left. How many children can go to the school altogether?

   d The whole school is going on a trip. Each coach can hold 72 people. How many coaches will the school need to book?

   e Everyone in the school brings £2 towards the trip. How much will the school have collected?

   f 75% of Keystage 2 children come to school by bus. How many children is that?

   g $\frac{1}{8}$ of Keystage 2 children bring packed lunch. How many children is that?

   h A sixth of the school were absent with the flu one week. How many children was that?

2 Make up 2 problems about Ingleton School for a friend to work out.

Refresher

Rosehill Infant School has 162 children.

a There are 48 children in Reception and 56 in Year 1. How many children is that?

b The rest of the children are in Year 2. How many children in Year 2?

c 50% of the children live less than 500 metres from the school. How many children is that?

d A third of the children have to come to school by car. How many children is that?

e All the children bring gloves to school one day. How many gloves in the school?

Challenge

1 a When Mum and her two children, Rose and Daisy, got on the scales, it showed 127 kg. When Daisy got off, it showed 103 kg. When Rose got off and Daisy got back on, it showed 89 kg. How much did Mum and her two children weigh?

b Selima and Becca took a job picking apples. Selima filled 4 buckets for every 3 that Becca filled. How many will Selima fill while Becca fills 24? What is the ratio of Selima's buckets to Becca's?

c Theo and Luke both start reading the same book on the same day. Theo reads 6 pages a day and Luke reads 9. What page will Luke be on when Theo is on Page 72? The book has 288 pages altogether. How many days will Theo take to read the book?

Square numbers

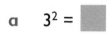

Practice

1 Complete each of the following.

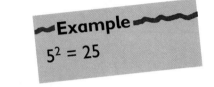

Example
$5^2 = 25$

a $3^2 = $ ☐

b $9^2 = $ ☐

c $7^2 = $ ☐

d $4^2 = $ ☐

e $12^2 = $ ☐

f $14^2 = $ ☐

g $8^2 = $ ☐

h $10^2 = $ ☐

i $13^2 = $ ☐

j $6^2 = $ ☐

k $5^2 = $ ☐

l $11^2 = $ ☐

2 Complete each of the following.

a ☐$^2 = 4$

b ☐$^2 = 121$

c ☐$^2 = 100$

d ☐$^2 = 169$

e ☐$^2 = 49$

f ☐$^2 = 64$

g ☐$^2 = 81$

h ☐$^2 = 144$

3 Complete each of the following.

a $6^2 + 4 = $ ☐

b $5^2 + 7 = $ ☐

c $12^2 + 9 = $ ☐

d $4^2 - 8 = $ ☐

e $8^2 - 12 = $ ☐

f $11^2 - 18 = $ ☐

g $3^2 + 16 = $ ☐

h $7^2 - 13 = $ ☐

i $9^2 + 19 = $ ☐

j $4^2 + 31 = $ ☐

k $5^2 - 19 = $ ☐

l $7^2 + 18 = $ ☐

Refresher

I Use the grid to help you find these square numbers.

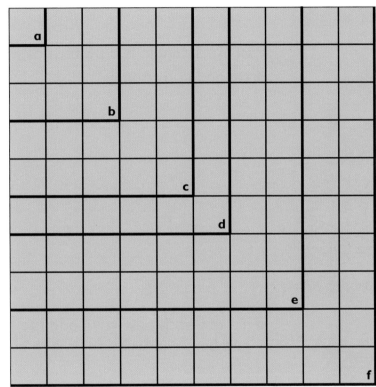

Challenge

I a $10^2 - 38 = \boxed{}$ b $11^2 + 23 = \boxed{}$ c $13^2 - 72 = \boxed{}$

d $12^2 - 46 = \boxed{}$ e $9^2 - 55 = \boxed{}$ f $8^2 + 37 = \boxed{}$

g $7^2 + 62 = \boxed{}$ h $20^2 + 52 = \boxed{}$

2 a $4^2 + 3^2 = \boxed{}$ b $5^2 + 6^2 = \boxed{}$ c $3^2 + 7^2 = \boxed{}$ d $6^2 - 3^2 = \boxed{}$

e $9^2 + 6^2 = \boxed{}$ f $8^2 - 5^2 = \boxed{}$ g $10^2 - 7^2 = \boxed{}$ h $9^2 - 4^2 = \boxed{}$

Triangular numbers

Practice

Pascal's triangle

Pascal was a French mathematician who lived in the 17th century.

Pascal's Triangle is a pattern of whole numbers arranged in a triangle.

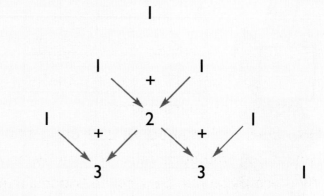

- To get each new row, add the two neighbouring numbers and write their sum between them on the row below.
- For example, 1 + 1 gives a sum of 2. 2 is written on the row below the two ones.
- The pattern goes on **forever**!

1 Complete your own Pascal's Triangle.

   Keep the Triangle going to see if you can find the numbers that are in the tenth row.

2 Look carefully at your Pascal's Triangle.

   Can you see any patterns?

3 a Write any patterns you can see. Explain how each pattern is developed.

  b Look at the first four diagonal lines. What is happening in each of these lines.

  c How can you use the patterns in each of these lines to check whether you have made a mistake?

  d Look at the diagonal line with the numbers 1, 3, 6, 10. What would the numbers in rows 11–15 be? How do you know?

Refresher

1 Copy and continue this pattern of dots to make a larger triangle.

Can you see any patterns?

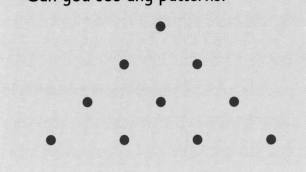

2 Draw a table to record your findings.

Row	Number of dots altogether	Number of dots added
1	1	1
2	3	2
3	6	3
4	...	...
...	...	...

3 Look carefully at your findings.

 a How does each number of dots altogether grow? Explain.

 b How many triangular numbers are there between 1 and 100?

 c Why are these numbers called triangular numbers?

 d Are there any triangular numbers that are also square numbers?

 e Are there any patterns relating to odd and even numbers?

Challenge

Use your Pascal's Triangle from the Practice Activity.

1 ● What if Pascal had started with 2 instead of 1. Would all of the numbers double?

 ● Keep the triangle going up to row 8. What patterns can you see?

2 ● What if Pascal had started his triangle with 1s along the base and worked upwards?

 ● What would the top number be?

 ● What patterns can you see?

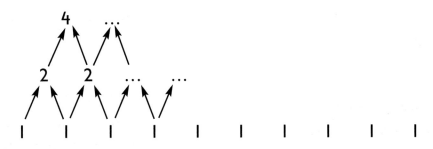

Investigating squares

Practice

The children in Year 6 carried out an investigation about making squares.

Investigation

- Use cm squared dot paper to make squares of different sizes.
- Make the squares by circling the dots around the outside of each side.
- Investigate the number of dots circled on the outside and the number of dots in the square on the inside.

The children drew their squares on dot paper.

Some children drew a table to help them record their results.

Size of inside square	Number of dots around the outside	Number of dots in the inside square
1 × 1	8	1
2 × 2	...	...
...	...	...
...	...	...

a Carry out your own investigation like the one above.
b Record your results clearly.
c Identify any patterns that appear.
d Explain why the patterns appear.

Refresher

1 Work out the rule for each sequence below.

2 Write the next 5 numbers in each sequence, then write the rule.

a 100, 104, 108, ☐ , ☐ , ☐ , ☐ , ☐ . The rule is ....

b 350, 355, 360, ☐ , ☐ , ☐ , ☐ , ☐ . The rule is ....

c −56, −53, −50, ☐ , ☐ , ☐ , ☐ , ☐ . The rule is ....

d −33, −22, −11, ☐ , ☐ , ☐ , ☐ , ☐ . The rule is ....

e 78, 90, 102, ☐ , ☐ , ☐ , ☐ , ☐ . The rule is ....

f 36, 45, 54, ☐ , ☐ , ☐ , ☐ , ☐ . The rule is ....

Challenge

Square number

Definition: *A whole number that is a product of a number and itself. For example, 9 is the square number made from 3 × 3 or 3 squared.*

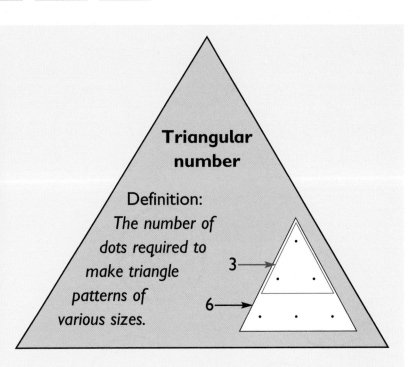

Triangular number

Definition: *The number of dots required to make triangle patterns of various sizes.*

3 →

6 →

Use your knowledge of square and triangular numbers to investigate this statement.

Any square number is the sum of 2 consecutive triangular numbers.

Counting patterns

Practice

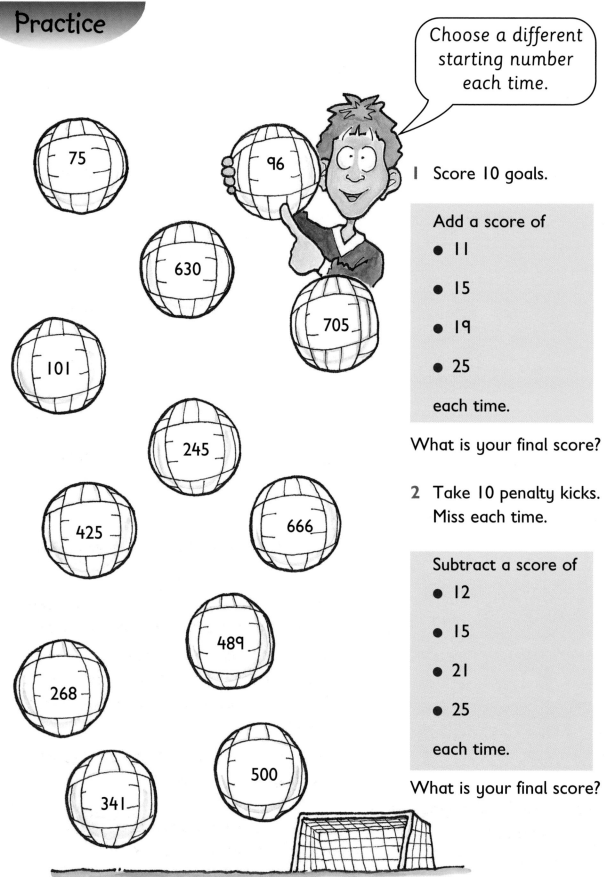

Choose a different starting number each time.

1 Score 10 goals.

Add a score of
- 11
- 15
- 19
- 25

each time.

What is your final score?

2 Take 10 penalty kicks. Miss each time.

Subtract a score of
- 12
- 15
- 21
- 25

each time.

What is your final score?

Refresher

1 Copy and complete the number sequences.
2 Write the rule.

a −34, −25, ▢, ▢, 2, 11, ▢, ▢, ▢, ▢. Rule: +9

b 15, 40, 65, ▢, ▢, ▢, ▢, ▢, ▢, ▢. Rule: ▢

c 361, ▢, ▢, 394, 405, ▢, ▢, ▢, ▢, ▢. Rule: ▢

d 652, ▢, ▢, ▢, 604, ▢, 580, 568, ▢, ▢. Rule: ▢

e −125, −150, −175, ▢, ▢, ▢, ▢, ▢, ▢, ▢. Rule: ▢

f −63, −72, ▢, ▢, ▢, −108, −117, ▢, ▢, ▢. Rule: ▢

g 36, ▢, ▢, 72, ▢, ▢, 108, ▢, ▢, 144. Rule: ▢

h −90, −75, ▢, ▢, ▢, ▢, 0, ▢, ▢, 45 Rule: ▢

Challenge

Types of number sequences

Add the previous two numbers.

Add or subtract the same number each time.

Multiply or divide the same number each time.

Add or subtract a changing number.

Combine 2 operations.

1 Which type of number sequence has been used for the Refresher and Practice activities?

2 For number sequences that require counting in steps of 11, 12, 15, 19 or 21, which types of number sequences would be appropriate to use?

3 Give two examples for each type of sequence you suggested in question 2.

Find the missing numbers

Practice

Here are some multiplication tables for you to try.

They are in code and each letter represents a different number.
(Each table has a different set of values for its letters.)

1 Can you work out which multiplication table belongs to
   each of the tables below?

2 Write an explanation of how you worked out your
   answer for each one.

Table □

A × K = K
A × S = S
A × Y = Y
A × F = F
A × A = A
A × L = L
A × B = B
A × G = G
A × M = M

Table △

Z × A = TL
Z × K = Z
Z × Z = DK
Z × B = NC
Z × N = KD
Z × C = AB
Z × D = CN
Z × L = BA
Z × T = LT

Table ○

S × A = FA
S × B = CD
S × C = G
S × D = CF
S × S = B
S × F = S
S × G = FJ
S × H = FC
S × J = CH

Table ◇

J × Z = UZ
J × Y = RQ
J × W = YT
J × V = TZ
J × U = J
J × J = RJ
J × S = TS
J × R = US
J × T = ZT

Refresher

$1\ 2\ 3\ 4\ 5\ 6\ 7\ 8\ 9\ 10$

Use the numbers 1–10 to make these statements correct.
For each number sentence a different letter indicates a
different number.

1. $A \times A = 16$
2. $B + B + B = 15$
3. $4 \times C = 24$
4. $D \times D = 30 + D$
5. $E + 25 = 34$
6. $F \times 15 = 30$
7. $G \times G \times G = 8$
8. $H + H + H = 9$

9. $J \times J \times J = J$
10. $K \times K + K = 110$
11. $40 - L - L - L - L = 0$
12. $M + M + M = N + N$
13. $P \times P = 72 - P$
14. $R \div 9 = S + S$
15. $T \times T + T = 42$
16. $V + V + V + V = 0$

Challenge

Valuable words

You may use a calculator where appropriate.

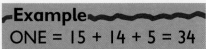

1. Write the letters A–Z in order.
2. Give each letter a number from 1 to 26 in order, so A = 1, B = 2, …
3. What is the sum of each of these words?

   EXPENSIVE   THOUSAND   AUTUMN   CHRISTMAS

   Example
   ONE = 15 + 14 + 5 = 34

4. What is the product of each of these words?

   TIMES   SUMMER   COMPUTE   MILLION

   Example
   ONE = 15 × 14 × 5 = 1050

5. Can you find a word that has a value of 100?
6. How many words can you find with a value of 1000?
   (You can mix operations and use brackets.)

Glossary

angles

right angle

acute angle

obtuse angle

180°   straight line

Angles are formed when two straight lines meet. We measure an **angle** by measuring the amount of turn from one line to the other.

Angles are measured in degrees. The symbol for degrees is °.

A right angle is 90 degrees, 90°. A right angle is shown by a small square.

An acute angle is less than 90°.

An obtuse angle is more than 90°.

A straight line has an angle of 180°. This can be used to work out the second angle.

See also protractor

arc

Any part of the circumference of a circle is called an **arc**.

See also circumference

area

Area is the amount of surface of a shape. It is measured in square centimetres. This can be abbreviated to cm².

You can work out the **area** of a rectangle by multiplying the length of the shape by the breadth. Length × breadth = **area**.

average

The **average** is the middle amount in any range of data.

You calculate the average by adding all the amounts then dividing by the number of items.

Marks in a maths test	
Joe 42	Average = 42 + 55 + 68 + 59 = 224
Sue 55	224 ÷ 4 = 56
Helen 68	The average score is 56
Sam 59	

Mean is another word for **average**.

axis, axes

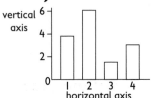

Graphs and charts have two **axes**.

The horizontal **axis** shows the range of data.
The vertical **axis** shows the frequency. They can be labelled in any equal divisions.

See also data

brackets

Brackets are used in maths for grouping parts of calculations together.

10 − (3 + 4) = 7
(10 − 3) + 4 = 11

The calculations in brackets need to be worked out first.

| | capacity | **Capacity** is the *amount* that something will hold. |

capacity

Capacity is the *amount* that something will hold.
Capacity is measured in litres and millilitres.
I litre is equal to 1000 millilitres.

Litre can be abbreviated to l.
Millilitres can be abbreviated to ml.

Capacity can also be measured in pints and gallons.

See imperial units

circumference

The **circumference** is the distance all the way round a circle.

column addition

When you add large numbers, using the standard vertical method can make the calculation easier.

The numbers must be written with the digits of the same place value underneath each other.

If the digits in one column add up to more than 9, the tens are carried to the next column.

column subtraction

Th	H	T	U
⁴5̷	¹7	¹2̷	5
− 3	8	0	6
1	9	1	9

When you subtract large numbers, using the standard vertical method can make the calculation easier.
The numbers must be written with the digits of the same place value underneath each other.

◄ If the top digit is lower than the bottom digit then 10 can be "borrowed" from the next column.

common denominator

A **common denominator** is when two or more fractions have the same denominator.

Fractions with different denominators need to be changed to have a **common denominator** before they can be added or subtracted.

$\frac{1}{2} + \frac{1}{4}$ can be changed to $\frac{2}{4} + \frac{1}{4}$

The **common denominator** is 4.

See also equivalent fraction

concentric

Concentric means *with the same centre*.
These circles are **concentric**.

co-ordinates

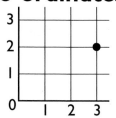

Co-ordinates are numbers or letters that help us to plot the exact position of something. We use them on maps, graphs or charts.

◄ Graphs like this are called the first quadrant.
On the graph, the dot is at (3, 2) 3 lines across and 2 lines up.
To read **co-ordinates** we look *across* and *up*. Some people remember this by thinking of "Along the corridor, up the stairs".

decimals

Decimal fractions show us the part of a number that is not a whole number.

The decimal point separates the whole numbers from the decimal fractions.

H	T	U •	ths	hdths
		5 •	8	
		5 •	8	6

◀ Each digit after the decimal point has a different place value.

5·8 is a number with one decimal place.
5·86 is a number with two decimal places.

Decimals and fractions

All decimals have a fraction equivalent. To find the decimal equivalent for a fraction we divide 1 by the denominator and then multiply by the numerator.

$\frac{3}{4} = 0.75$
$1 \div 4 = 0.25$
$0.25 \times 3 = 0.75$

$\frac{1}{2} = 0.5$
$\frac{1}{4} = 0.25$
$\frac{3}{4} = 0.75$
$\frac{1}{10} = 0.1$
$\frac{3}{10} = 0.3$
$\frac{1}{5} = 0.2$
$\frac{1}{100} = 0.01$
$\frac{3}{100} = 0.03$

See also fractions

divisibility

There are some quick tests you can do to see if one number will divide by another.

You can use your knowledge of multiplication facts: $3 \times 4 = 12$ so 12 is divisible by 3 and 4.

Other tests:

2s   Any even number is divisible by 2.

4s   If you can divide the last two digits of the number by 4 exactly, the whole number will divide exactly by 4. 216 is divisible by 4 as 16 is divisible by 4.

5s   You can divide 5 exactly into any number ending in 5 or 0.

10s   If a number ends in 0 you can divided it by 10 exactly.

100s   If a number ends in two zeros it will divide exactly by 100.

1000s   Any number that ends in three zeros is divisible by 1000.

dividing by 10, 100 and 1000	When a number is **divided by 10, 100 or 1000** the digits move one, two or three place values to the right. If the hundreds, tens and units digit is zero it disappears, if it is not zero it becomes a decimal. The place value of the digits decreases 10, 100 or 1000 times. *See also* multiplying by 10, 100 and 1000
dodecahedron	A **dodecahedron** is a solid shape with 12 faces. The faces are pentagons.
equivalent fractions	**Equivalent fractions** are fractions of equal value. They are worth the same. $\frac{4}{8}$ is equivalent to $\frac{1}{2}$ *See also* common denominator *See also* fractions
factor	A **factor** is a whole number which will divide exactly into another whole number. The factors of 12 are 1, 2, 3, 4, 6, 12 as they all divide into 12. The factors can be put into pairs. If the pairs are multiplied together they will equal 12. 1×12 2×6 3×4
formula	A **formula** is a way of writing down a rule. For example, to find the area of a rectangle you multiply the length by the width.
fractions	**Fractions** are parts of something. $\frac{1}{2}$ →numerator →denominator The numerator tells you how many parts we are talking about. The denominator tells you how many parts the whole has been split into.
fractions and division	We find fractions of amounts by dividing by the denominator and then multiplying by the numerator. We divide by the denominator as this is the number of parts the amount needs to be divided into. We then multiply by the numerator as this is the number of parts we are talking about. *See also* fractions

imperial units
These used to be the standard measurements in Britain. They have now been replaced by metric units. Some imperial units are still used today.

Capacity
1 pint = 0·568 l
8 pints = 1 gallon

Mass
1 ounce (oz) = 28·35 g
1 pound (lb) = 16 ounces

Length
1 yard = 0·914 m
1 mile = 1·6 km
1 inch = 2·54 cm
1 foot = 0·305 m

improper fraction
An **improper fraction** is a fraction where the numerator is more than the denominator.

$\frac{13}{5}$

These are sometimes called top heavy fractions.
Improper fractions can be changed to whole numbers or mixed numbers.

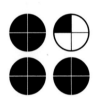

◄ $\frac{5}{4} = 1\frac{1}{4}$

◄ $\frac{8}{4} = 2$

A fraction that is not an **improper fraction** is a proper fraction.

See also fractions
See also mixed numbers

integer
Integer is another name for a whole number.

See also whole number

intersection
If two lines **intersect** they cross each other.

These lines intersect at **A**.
A is the point of intersection.

inverse operations
Inverse means *the opposite operation*. The **inverse operation** will undo the first operation.

Addition and subtraction are **inverse operations**:
17 + 26 = 43   43 − 26 = 17

Multiplication and division are **inverse operations**:
6 × 9 = 54   54 ÷ 9 = 6

length
Length is how long an object or a distance is.
Length is measured in kilometres, metres, centimetres and millimetres.

1 kilometre is equal to 1000 metres.
1 metre is equal to 100 centimetres.
1 centimetre is equal to 10 millimetres.

Kilometre can be abbreviated to km.
Metre can be abbreviated to m.
Centimetre can be abbreviated to cm.
Millimetre can be abbreviated to mm.

Length can also be measured in miles.

See also imperial units

long division

When you divide numbers which are too large to work out mentally, you can use **long division**. We call it **long division** when both numbers involved are two digits or more.

long multiplication

		3	5	2
×			2	7
	7	0	4	0
	2	4	6	4
	9	5	0	4
		1		

When you multiply numbers which are too large to work out mentally, you can use **long multiplication**. We call it **long multiplication** when both numbers involved are more than a single-digit.

The numbers must be written with the digits of the same place value underneath each other.

See also short multiplication

mass

Mass is another word for weight.
Mass is measured in grams and kilograms.
1 kilogram is equal to 1000 grams.
Mass can be measured in pounds and ounces.

See also imperial units

mean

Mean is another word for average.

See also average

median

The **median** of a range of data is the item that comes *halfway*.

> Marks in a maths test
>
> 46   51   52   (60)   62   65   71
>
> 60 is the **median**.

mode

The **mode** of a set of data is the number that occurs most often.

multiplication

Multiplication is the inverse operation to division.
Numbers can be multiplied in any order and the answer will be the same.
$5 \times 9 = 45$ $9 \times 5 = 45$

See also inverse operations

multiplying by 10, 100 and 1000

Th	H	T	U
		2	3
	2	3	0

23 × 10 = 230

Our number system is based around 10.
When a number is **multiplied by 10, 100 or 1000** the digits move one, two or three place values to the left and zeros go in the empty column to keep its place value.

◄ The place value of the digits increases 10, 100 or 1000 times.

See also dividing by 10, 100 and 1000

multiples

A **multiple** is a number that can be divided into another number.

2, 4, 6, 8, 10, 12 are all **multiples** of 2 as we can divide 2 into them all.

10, 20, 30, 40, 50, 60, 70 are all **multiples** of 10 as we can divide 10 into them all.

Multiples can be recognised by using the multiplication facts.

See also multiplication facts

negative numbers

Numbers and integers can be positive or **negative**.
Negative integers or numbers are *below* zero.

Negative numbers have a minus sign before them.
–56

Negative numbers are ordered in the same way as positive numbers except they run from right to left.

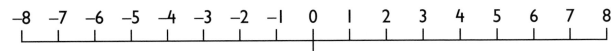

See also positive numbers

net

A **net** is a flat shape which can be cut out and folded up to make a solid shape.

<, >, ≤, ≥

are symbols used to order numbers.

< means less than   45<73
> means more than   73>45
≤ means less than or equal to   45≤45, 44
≥ means more than or equal to 87≥87, 88

ordering fractions

When you **order fractions** and mixed numbers, first look at the whole numbers then the fractions. If the fractions have different denominators, think about the fractions in relation to a half to help you to order them.

parallel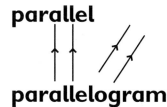

Parallel lines are lines that are the same distance apart all the way along.

◄ They are often shown by two little arrows.

parallelogram

A **parallelogram** is a four-sided shape with its opposite sides parallel to each other.

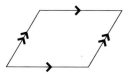

percentage

The sign % stands for *per cent*, which means out of 100.
30% means 30 out of 100.

Percentages are linked to fractions and decimals.
$\frac{1}{2}$ = 50% = 0·5
$\frac{1}{4}$ = 25% = 0·25
$\frac{3}{4}$ = 75% = 0·75
$\frac{1}{5}$ = 20% = 0·2
$\frac{1}{10}$ = 10% = 0·10

Finding percentages of amounts

To find **percentages** of amounts we need to use the relationship to fractions.

To find 50% of an amount, we divide by 2: 50% = $\frac{1}{2}$.
50% of £40 is £20.

To find 25% we divide by 4: 25% = $\frac{1}{4}$
To find 20% we divide by 5: 20% = $\frac{1}{5}$

perpendicular

A **perpendicular** line meets another line at right angles.

perimeter

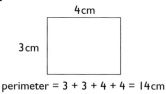

perimeter = 3 + 3 + 4 + 4 = 14cm

Perimeter is the distance all the way around a flat shape.

You can calculate the **perimeter** of a shape by adding the length of all the sides together.

If a shape has sides all the same length then you can use multiplication to work out the **perimeter**.

pie chart

A **pie chart** is a way of showing information.

Y6 journeys to school

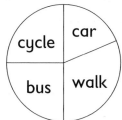

plane

A **plane** is a flat surface.

prime factor   A **prime factor** is a factor which is also a prime number.

See also prime number

See also factor

prime number   **Prime numbers** are numbers that can only be divided by 1 and themselves.

A prime number has only two factors.

17 is a prime number. It can only be divided exactly by 1 and 17.

1 is not counted as a prime number.

The prime numbers to 20 are:

2, 3, 5, 7, 11, 13, 19

probability   **Probability** is about how *likely* or *unlikely* the outcome of an event is. The event may be the throw of a die or whether or not it will rain today.

We use certain words to discuss **probability**. We can put events and the words on a scale from *no chance of it happening* to *certain*.

| impossible | | | even | possibly | good | |
| no chance | unlikely | | chance | likely | chance | certain |

Even chance means an event is as likely to happen as not happen.

product   **Product** is another name for the answer to a multiplication calculation.

24 is the product of 6 × 4

proportion   **Proportion** shows the relationship between two connected things.

When amounts are being compared and they have equal ratios they are in **proportion**.

1 packet of biscuits costs 60p
2 packets of biscuits cost £1·20
3 packets cost £1·80
The cost is in **proportion** to the number of packets bought.

See also ratio

quadrant   A **quadrant** is a quarter of a circle.

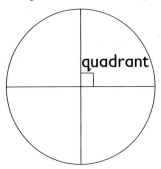

Quadrants are used in graphs.

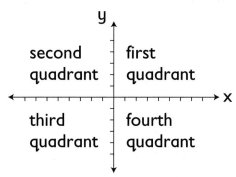

quotient

Quotient is another name for the answer to a division calculation.

The remainder of the **quotient** can be shown as a fraction or a decimal fraction.

$27 \div 4 = 6 \text{ r } 3$
$27 \div 4 = 6\frac{3}{4}$
$27 \div 4 = 6 \cdot 75$

As we are dividing by 4, the fraction will be a quarter and there are 3 of them left. 0·75 is the decimal equivalent to $\frac{3}{4}$.

range

The **range** of a set of data is the lowest to the highest value.

ratio

Ratio is a way of comparing amounts or numbers.

It can be used in two ways:

It can describe the relationship between *part to whole*.
A cake is divided into 4 equal parts and one part is eaten. The **ratio** of part to whole is one part in every four parts or 1 in 4.

Or it can describe the relationship of *part to other part*.
A cake is divided into 4 parts and one part is eaten. The ratio of part to part is 1 to 3 as for every piece eaten three pieces are left.

The **ratio** 1 to 3 can also be written as 1:3.

See also proportion

reflection

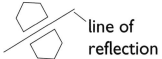
line of reflection

◀ If a shape is **reflected**, it is drawn as it would appear reflected in a mirror held against or alongside one of its sides.

reflective symmetry

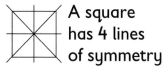
A square has 4 lines of symmetry

A shape is symmetrical if both sides are the same when a line is drawn through the shape. The line can be called a mirror line or an axes.

◀ Some shapes have more than one line of symmetry.

rhombus

A **rhombus** is a four-sided shape. Its sides are all equal in length. The opposite sides are parallel.

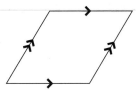

round number

A **round number** usually ends in a zero. When using or estimating with large numbers round numbers are easier to work with.

short division

When you divide numbers that are too large to work out mentally, you can use **short division**. We call it **short division** when one of the numbers involved is a single-digit.

short multiplication

When you multiply numbers that are too large to work mentally, you can use **short multiplication**. We call it **short multiplication** when one of the numbers involved is a single-digit.

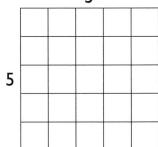

◀ The numbers must be written with the digits of the same place value underneath each other.

See also long multiplication

square numbers

To **square** a number it is multiplied by itself. The answer is a **square number**.

To square 5, we multiply 5 by itself. 25 is the **square number**.

◀ $5 \times 5 = 25$ can also be written as $5^2 = 25$

Square numbers have an odd number of factors. The factors of 25 are 1, 5, 25.

Square numbers up to 100

$1 \times 1 = \textbf{1}$
$2 \times 2 = \textbf{4}$
$3 \times 3 = \textbf{9}$
$4 \times 4 = \textbf{16}$
$5 \times 5 = \textbf{25}$
$6 \times 6 = \textbf{36}$
$7 \times 7 = \textbf{49}$
$8 \times 8 = \textbf{64}$
$9 \times 9 = \textbf{81}$
$10 \times 10 = \textbf{100}$

See also factor

symmetrical pattern

Patterns can be **symmetrical**. They may have two lines of symmetry.

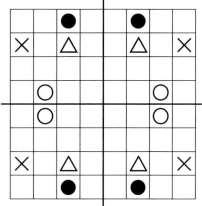

line of symmetry

line of symmetry

time

These are the units **time** is measured in:
seconds
minutes
hours
days
weeks
months
years

These are the relationships between these units:
60 seconds = 1 minute
60 minutes = 1 hour
24 hours = 1 day
7 days = 1 week
4 weeks = 1 month
12 months = 1 year
365 days = 1 year

analogue   digital
clock   clock

◀ **Time** can be read on analogue clocks or digital clocks.

Digital clocks can be 12 hour or 24 hour.
The 12-hour clock uses a.m. and p.m.
The 24-hour clock carries on after 12 o'clock midday to 24 instead of starting at 1 again.

translation

A **translation** is when a shape is moved by sliding it.

trapezium

A **trapezium** is a four sided shape with two parallel sides.

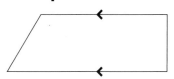

triangles

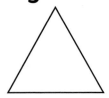

A **triangle** is a 2D shape with three straight sides and three angles.

There are four kinds of triangle:

Equilateral triangle
◀ This has three equal sides and three equal angles.

Isosceles triangle
◀ This has two equal sides. The angles opposite these two sides are also equal.

Scalene triangle
◀ All three sides are different lengths.
The angles are all different too.

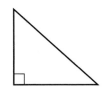

Right-angled triangle
◀ This has one right angle.

vertex

The **vertex** is the tip or top of a shape, the point furthest away from the base. The plural is **vertices**.

x is the **vertex** of the cone

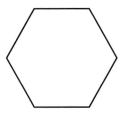

A regular hexagon has 6 vertices